FOREVER WILD

FOREVER WILD

Maine's Magnificent Baxter State Park

Text and Photographs by
ROBERT VILLANI

DOWN EAST BOOKS

For my wife, Miriam

ISBN 0-89272-306-8
Library of Congress Catalog Card Number 91-74035
Book design by Janet Patterson
Color separations, printing, and binding
    done in Hong Kong through Four Colour Imports

5   4   3   2   1

Down East Books
P.O. Box 679
Camden, Maine 04843

Contents

Preface

A mountain maple (Acer spicatum) *in autumn colors at the edge of a marshy area near Daicey Pond. In the distance is cloud-covered Mount Katahdin.*

My first visit to Baxter State Park in 1980 was a momentous occasion: I was completing a backpack of the Appalachian Trail, headed for its northern terminus at Baxter Peak, the summit of Baxter State Park's Mount Katahdin. Starting in Georgia's Chattahoochie Mountains, more than two thousand miles south of Katahdin, I made my way northward. Katahdin was always on my mind because it represented my final destination, but Baxter State Park's reputation as the trail's finest wilderness was an even greater enticement.

As I followed the trail into the Park, it lead to Daicey Pond, one of the area's loveliest bodies of water. Mount Katahdin, rising abruptly from the low land to the east, cast its subtle reflection down onto the surface of the pond. Gazing across the water, contemplating the mountain I would climb the next day, I realized that Baxter State Park not only had met my expectations but even ex-

ceeded them. Katahdin's massive silhouette was magnetic, compelling me to explore it further.

So began my love affair with the Park. Since then I have returned many times to Baxter, exploring Mount Katahdin and the Park's many other equally enchanting virtues.

Baxter State Park has had a similar mesmerizing effect on many who have visited it. Long before the Park itself was

established in 1933, an array of notable figures visited this realm. Katahdin inspired Henry David Thoreau, for example, to write some of the most reflective and graphic passages in his essay, "In the Maine Woods." In more recent times, this land compelled Maine Governor Percival Proctor Baxter to methodically amass parcels of acreage that he eventually donated to the state of Maine to establish the Park.

A cow moose (Alces alces) *feeds in Sandy Stream Pond as sunrise illuminates the snow-capped Katahdin massif.*

Mount Katahdin rises over the waters of Mink Pond in the Park's southern section.

The story of Baxter State Park's preservation is an interesting and perhaps unparalleled account of one man's obsession and extraordinary foresight. Much has been written about it and the many other aspects of human history connected with this land. This book briefly discusses those fascinating aspects, but it focuses primarily on the Park's natural treasures.

Most visitors to the Park tend to center their activities on Katahdin, its most prominent feature. Katahdin is an unrivaled natural wonder, but the Park abounds with other attributes deserving equal attention. Over the years, and in every season, I have explored the Park's varied habitats, climbed its numerous peaks, and observed its bountiful wildlife. Through the text and photographs that follow, I hope to acquaint the reader with the various ecosystems, the flora and fauna, and the spectacular vistas found within the Park's borders.

Baxter State Park offers incomparable mountain scenery along with a truly undeveloped wilderness setting— two extremely rare commodities in the exceedingly congested eastern United States. The Park is a place where personal limits can be tested on a precipitous, boulder-strewn trail; where enthralling panoramas can be viewed from a spectacular peak; or where a cow moose and her calf can be observed dining on succulent aquatic vegetation. Baxter State Park has something to offer all of its visitors, no matter what their outdoor interests, in a setting where limited human access forever preserves a wilderness state.

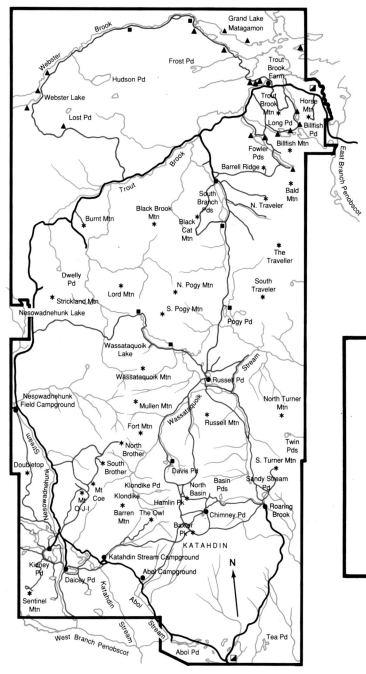
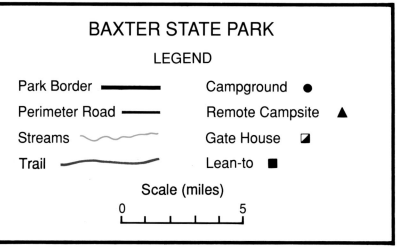

The Park:
An Overview

*Stump Pond, near the Park Perimeter Road,
is a favorite haunt of moose. The peaks
in the distance include Mount Coe, Barren,
and O-J-I.*

Envision a large tract of land in the densely populated northeastern section of the United States—a place free of most of the trappings associated with decades of industrial development and expansion. Imagine a place where nature is the only force that shapes its countenance; where flora and fauna are limited only by the carrying capacities of their habitats; where the water runs clean and clear and the air has a crystal vigor. Such a place is Baxter State Park.

Located in north-central Maine, Baxter is one of the nation's largest state parks, encompassing more than two hundred thousand acres. Undeveloped land surrounding the Park—primarily owned by paper companies for logging—acts as a woodland buffer of millions of acres around the Park's perimeter. Despite the remoteness of this area, however access by automobile is relatively easy. The Park's southern entrance is seventeen miles north of the town of Millinocket, and not far from Interstate 95. The Park's northern entrance at Grand Lake Matagamon, near the town of Patten, also is easily accessible from Interstate 95. Baxter is one-half to a full day's drive from most metropolitan centers in the Northeast. The combination

of easy access and a unique natural heritage of unspoiled wilderness makes Baxter one of the most important protected lands in this part of the country.

The southern (and most-used) entrance to the Park is at Togue Pond Gate. Here the Park Perimeter Road commences, following the old Nesowadnehunk Tote Road for half its distance. The road is unpaved, narrow, and winding, a little-changed remnant of the region's early history as an important logging center. It extends more than fifty miles from the Park's south gate to the north gate, and, other than its several short spurs leading to campgrounds, is the Park's only path for vehicular traffic.

In keeping with the Park's "forever wild" philosophy, there are no special provisions for sight-seeing motorists, such as National Park–style scenic lookouts. There are several picnic areas, however, usually with a mountain stream as a water source and a pit toilet. Many of these are located near trail heads. Numerous and well maintained foot trails lead to a variety of scenic spots. These wilderness paths are the best way to experience Baxter's many offerings.

Long before today's hikers and campers explored the land that became

the Park, native Americans trod its turf. It is believed that there were no permanent Indian settlements in the Katahdin area, but the region was visited regularly by tribes of the Abenaki Nation, who had several settlements along the Penobscot River to the south. The Abenakis, whose activities were more focused along the coast of Maine, would visit the inland area during hunting forays and en route to visit other tribes in the St. Lawrence River Valley.

In the traditions of many native American tribes, mountains were regarded as sacred lands where ancestors' spirits and other powerful deities resided. The Abenakis were no exception, and they appropriately chose Katahdin, the largest and most awe-inspiring mountain in their territory, as one of the centers of their spiritual world. Three spirits made Katahdin their home. Of humanoid form with a stony countenance, and regarded as the most powerful of the three, was an omnipotent benign being referred to as the "spirit of Katahdin." There was also a spirit of neutral demeanor named Wuchowen, known as the "spirit of the night wind." Wuchowen possessed great wings that he used to create the forest breezes. The third was a dangerous,

A rainbow crowns the cloud-covered summit of Mount Katahdin as viewed from Daicey Pond.

Machiavellian spirit. Over time, white men settling in the area fused these three gods into one powerful being. Embodying the attributes of the evil spirit, this god was elevated to the position of supreme spirit of Katahdin and given the name Pamola (taken from *Bumole*, the Indian name for him). Pamola, in keeping with his Indian origins, was described as being a birdlike creature with grossly exaggerated beak and claws. He was said to be the harbinger of violent storms, lashing out at anyone who too closely approached his domain.

Today the Indians' beliefs have all but faded away, and with thousands of hikers climbing Mount Katahdin each year, it seems that Pamola is no longer so feared. The most evident legacy of the Abenaki are the many colorful Indian names in Baxter State Park. *Katahdin* is the most familiar example. Taken from the Indian name *Kette-Adene*, it means "greatest mountain." Over the years, the name has gone through a variety of other forms, such as *Taddn, Ktahdin, Ktaahden,*

Ktaadn, and *Katadin.* Examples of the many other Indian names still used in the Park are *Nesowadnehunk*, meaning "swift stream in the mountains"; *Wassa-taquoik*, "a clear, shining lake"; and *Abol*, "bare, devoid of trees."

The migration of white men to this region began during the nineteenth century. A number of explorers, scien-tists, and sportsmen came to experience the wonders of Katahdin, but by far the greatest impetus bringing people to the region was the expanding lumber in-dustry. Like the Indians, early visitors to the area came by way of the West Branch of the Penobscot River. They would follow the river to the Abol Deadwater, its closest point to Katahdin,

White-tailed deer (Odocoileus virginianus) —here, a buck in velvet—also frequent the Park's ponds in search of aquatic delicacies.

Water drips from the muzzle of a cow moose (Alces alces) as she feeds on aquatic vegetation in Sandy Stream Pond.

where the Penobscot converges with two mountain streams the Indians knew as *Aboljackarnegassic* and *Aboljecarmegus*. Simplified by white men, these names became Abol Stream and Katahdin Stream.

Visitors made their way along Abol Stream to the site of the Abol Slide, at the base of Katahdin. The Abol Slide of 1816 left a long open gash on the southwest side of the mountain. Rock slides were desirable for climbers because they cleared a path through dense scrub on the mountain's upper reaches that often made an ascent tedious, if not impossible. The Abol Slide, visible from the river, was a logical route for most climbers.

*Orange Hawkweed (*Hieracium auran-tiacum*) and Mouse-ear Hawkweed (*Hieracium pilosella*) are two nonnative species that probably colonized the Park with the arrival of lumbering. In midsummer, they often form impressive carpets of colorful blooms in fields and disturbed areas along the Park Perimeter Road.*

Charles Turner, Jr., and a party of surveyors from Massachusetts were the first white men known to have reached Katahdin's summit. Although they reached the summit on August 13, 1804, twelve years prior to the Abol Slide, it is believed this party scaled the cliffs near where the slide occurred. In subsequent years, the Penobscot's West Branch and the Abol Slide became the most popular route to Katahdin's summit.

Henry David Thoreau reached the summit in 1846 by way of the West Branch. Thoreau's perceptive descriptions of Katahdin's scenic virtues in his essay "The Maine Woods" did much to publicize the attractiveness of this land. It was the first authentic description of the area. Furthermore, his insightful discussion of the lumberman's existence serves as an important window on a life-style now lost. At the time of Thoreau's

visit, lumbering already was changing the shape of this virgin wilderness.

By the mid-nineteenth century, the difficult and time-consuming West Branch approach to Katahdin was being replaced by another route from the east. Rail and stage lines began operations and reached their terminus in Stacyville, Maine. It then became possible to use the multitude of lumber roads being cut on the eastern side of Katahdin. In 1848, the Reverend Marcus R. Keep opened the first blazed trail up the mountain. It ran from Katahdin Lake to the base of what is now known as the Avalanche Slide and then climbed to the top of Pamola Peak. Within a short time, this approach was obliterated by a large-scale lumber operation.

Lumbering in what is now Baxter State Park was extensive, and it left vestiges that are still visible. To make these ventures practical, operations of the time centered on waterways that could be used for running logs. Within the Park area were five streams that suited this purpose. The first was Nesowadnehunk Stream, on the western side of the Park. (As mentioned earlier, the associated Nesowadnehunk Tote Road is still used as the major portion of the Park's Perimeter Road.) The second waterway utilized was Sandy Stream, east of Katahdin. The third was Wassataquoik Stream, in the Park's central region. Trout Brook in the north and Webster Lake and Stream near the Park's northern borders were the other waterways used by the lumber companies.

Most of these waterways were not suitable for log running until they were altered. So numerous dams were constructed in order to raise water levels and provide swift propulsion for the logs. Remnants of many of these dams are visible today. Two examples are the Toll Dam near Little Niagara Falls on the Appalachian Trail, and Sandy Stream Pond—on which a western outlet was blasted out to bypass its natural outlet at the eastern end and create a quicker route to Roaring Brook. Probably the most extensive alteration to the natural flow of water occurred at Telos Lake, which lies outside the Park boundary. The water in Telos, Chamberlain, Churchill, and Eagle lakes ran north by way of the Allagash and St. John rivers into Canada's St. Lawrence. This made it impossible for Maine companies to use those waters for removing timber. To rectify this, a canal (known today as the Telos cut) was built between Telos Lake and a neighboring ravine. A dam was also constructed to raise the water in Telos Lake, allowing it to drain in the opposite direction into Webster Lake and down Webster Stream, ultimately running into the East Branch of the Penobscot.

Lumbering flourished from about 1830 through 1968, touching on almost all parts of the present-day park. A small area at the head of Howe Brook near The Traveler escaped the axman's blows, as did other small parcels that are at higher elevations and have proved inaccessible. The only significant region left in its virgin state is The Klondike, a vast, flat bowl of spruce lying between Katahdin to the east and Barren, O-J-I, Coe, and The Brothers to the west. (O-J-I was named for three prominent landslides on the mountain's southwestern slope that once formed the three letters O, J, and I.) The Klondike, although a tempting prize for the lumberjacks, thoroughly embodied the very essence of Baxter Park: wilderness. Too wild and unyielding an area to produce a profit, The Klondike was left untouched.

The extensive lumbering in this area sparked construction of a maze of roads. Some led to lumber camps and were relatively permanent, such as the Nesowad-nehunk and Wassataquoik tote roads. Others were more transitory, cut only to reach timber. This network of woods roads also offered easy access for sportsmen and explorers, and new routes were cut to the summit of Katahdin, many of which are part of today's trail network. Beginning in the early 1900s, a number of sporting camps were established to cater to tourists who wanted to hike or hunt. Two of the most notable camps were located at Daicey Pond and Kidney Pond. Today, Baxter State Park utilizes structures from these camps as wilderness cabins for overnight guests.

William F. Tracy set up another sporting camp at Russell Pond, in what is now the central part of the Park. William's relative, Foster J. Tracy, along with his son-in-law, Hugh Love, were the principals of the logging firm of Tracy and Love. Although limited timber harvesting began in this area in the 1840s, Tracy and Love in 1883 initiated what was the first of four large-scale lumbering operations. In 1885, the Tracy and Love Trail to the top of Katahdin was cleared. Extending from Wassata-quoik Stream south, between Tip Top and Russell mountains, to Howe Peaks

on Katahdin, this trail was later used by guests at the Russell Pond Camps. Nowadays, the North Peaks Trail follows this same path. Long before the Tracy and Love Trail was cut, this became the preferred route to Katahdin's summit. The first party to use it was that of Edward Everett Hale, who reached the summit in 1845, followed by the Aaron Young Botanical Survey party in 1847. This was the second route to be exploited after the Abol Slide approach.

The vast amount of timber in the area around Russell Pond spurred extensive harvesting operations, and support communities sprang up along the Wassataquoik Tote Road, which followed Wassataquoik Stream to the East Branch of the Penobscot River. Also along this road was the first lumber camp within what is now the park boundary—called Old City—located at the convergence of Pogy Brook and Wassataquoik Stream.

Just south of Russell Pond, between Turner Brook and Wassataquoik Stream, was the site of New City, a rather large lumber camp complete with a school, church, and blacksmith shop. The present-day Tracy Horse Trail passes through what is now only a landscape of large fields slowly being reclaimed by the

forest. Yet evidence of the old camp exists in the many still-visible foundations. Sharp-eyed hikers can also spot old tools and implements scattered about.

In addition to these large camps, there were smaller ones, such as those at Russell Pond and Annis Brook. As in other areas in the Park, a number of dams were constructed in what became the Park's central region, to raise water levels. In order to further facilitate the removal of timber, a large sluice was built from the top of Pogy Mountain down to Wassataquoik Lake. Tip Top Mountain to the south also had a sluice, but it was not quite as large as the Pogy Mountain structure, which required a huge, trestle-type support. By 1914, the Draper operation, the largest and last of the lumbering enterprises in this area, ceased. This brought to an end the cutting of wood around Russell Pond.

Before the loggers withdrew, several major forest fires struck the area. The largest was the great Wassataquoik fire of 1903, which swept through Pogy Notch, where air funnelling through the valley stoked the blaze to great intensity The conflagration quickly engulfed the bowl of land around Russell Pond, wiping out forest and lumber camp alike.

Baxter State Park's winters are long and severe. Weeks of subzero temperatures freeze solid most of the Park's ponds. Here, the snag of a weathered Red Spruce (Picea rubens) emerges from a snow-covered island on Kidney Pond. The mountains in the distance are Doubletop and O-J-I.

Partridgeberry (Mitchella repens), a creeping evergreen vine, produces small red fruit in autumn. It is common in the Park and often forms dense mats on the forest floor.

Clouds forming over Baxter Peak in late afternoon. Without warning, Katahdin's unpredictable weather can turn a perfectly clear day into a fog-dominated washout.

A woodchuck (Marmota monax) suns itself on a warm rock near the entrance to its burrow. Woodchucks are found most often in the open areas along the Park Perimeter Road.

FOREVER WILD

Rapids on Nesowadnehunk Stream, with O-J-I Mountain in the distance. Visible in the stream are the wooden remains of the Toll Dam built during the logging era.

was no reason to maintain wild lands in a state that already was predominantly rural. Opposition from the timber industry, among others, also loomed.

It was then that Governor Baxter made the unprecedented decision to use his own funds to acquire the property personally. After increasing his worth through the wise acquisition of stocks and bonds, he set out to achieve his objective. In 1930, he made his first purchase, procuring nearly six thousand acres of some of the finest wilderness in the eastern United States. This remarkable initial parcel included most of the Mount Katahdin complex. The following year, he donated the land to the state. Anchored to this magnanimous gift was an exacting series of stipulations calling for the state to accept the land only on condition that a special management plan designed by Baxter would be implemented.

The governor adamantly required that three conditions be met. The first

was that the Park shall continue in its "natural wild state" and remain a wilderness for all time. The second was that the Park should remain a "sanctuary for wild birds and beasts," forever protecting the native wildlife. The third condition was that the Park "shall be held by the State in trust forever," allowing for limited recreational purposes such as

A male bobolink (Dolichonyx oryzivorus) singing in the fields at Trout Brook Farm where this species nests each year.

Sunrise lights up the woods near Roaring Brook after an early autumn snowfall.

Abol Mountain and its colorful autumn hardwoods, viewed from Abol Pond, are dwarfed by Katahdin's barren profile.

hiking, camping, and canoeing. Motorized devices would be prohibited in the Park, except for automobiles,* and the only automobile road would be the Park Perimeter Road, which had to remain forever an unpaved, primitive route. Additionally, it was stipulated that electric and water lines would not be built within Park borders. Even today, only primitive facilities exist for visitors.

---

*Winter visitors began exploring the Park on snowmobiles during the 1960s, and in 1969 the Park imposed restrictions on the use of those machines. The restrictions stood until 1977, when snowmobile traffic was completely banned except for Park administrative uses or emergencies. The Maine Snowmobile Association and other citizens' groups quickly challenged the ban in court, and the resulting Maine Supreme Court decision once again allows limited use of snowmobiles on portions of the Perimeter Road.

Weathered dead trees fill the shallow waters of the Littlefield Deadwater, near Trout Brook. Deadwaters are slow-moving, murky sections of streams that are excellent places to watch moose (and be eaten alive by insects).

A red maple (Acer rubrum) *branch in fiery fall colors droops over a clear mountain spring.*

Winter's white blankets Hamlin Peak and Hamlin Ridge along the headwall of the North Basin.

Furthermore, there is a limit on the number of people permitted into the Park at any one time, and pets are not allowed. As may be surmised from this abbreviated list of the rules, recreational activities in the Park are secondary to the Park's basic principle of maintaining a "natural wild state."

In later years, Governor Baxter secured additional acreage, purchasing some of it by allowing the seller to retain certain rights for a period of time. Most of these arrangements were with timber companies, which continued harvesting within the allotted time frame. The last of those rights ended in 1973, since

which time the Baxter State Park Authority has maintained all rights to the Park with the exception of certain water rights on Webster and Matagamon lakes.

Several of Baxter's later land purchases deviated from the governor's primary "forever wild" prerequisites in that the harvesting of wood was still allowed on 28,534 acres between the Perimeter Road and the Park's north and west borders. The governor authorized this for several reasons. First, there was a growing concern among local inhabitants that too much wood in this part of the state was being placed out of reach, to the potential detriment of the area's economy. Second, Governor Baxter wanted to create an area of "scientific forestry practices" where timber would be cut for profit but experimentation also could be carried out to find ways to improve harvesting techniques.

Baxter donated the scientific forestry area to the state in 1955, and harvesting

Katahdin at sunset, reflected on the surface of Tracy Pond.

Clouds fill the cirque of the North Basin one autumn morning.

began in 1978. Almost immediately, a protest arose over the logging practices being used. A citizens' organization calling itself the Scientific Forestry Area Advisory Group brought enough pressure to bear that the Park suspended harvesting until a better management plan could be developed that was more in line with Governor Baxter's original intent. Cutting resumed in 1989.

The governor also made an exception in his "sanctuary for wild birds and beasts" stipulation by allowing hunting on two parcels of land. He did this in order to appease the hunting interests, which were dependent on harvesting game or guiding hunters into the area as sources of income. One hunting area roughly encompasses the same land as that of the scientific forestry domain. The second area where the governor provided for hunting was part of his final purchase. In 1962, at the age of eighty-three, he bought a 7,764-acre parcel that included Abol and Togue ponds, near the

Park's southern entrance. Over a period of thirty-two years, Governor Baxter had acquired and given to the state a total of 201,018 acres, which an indebted State Legislature had gratefully named Baxter State Park in 1933.

The Park operates under the auspices of a state agency, the Baxter State Park Authority. It has three members: the Maine attorney general (appointed by the state legislature), the director of the Bureau of Forestry, and the commissioner of Inland Fisheries and Wildlife (both appointed by the governor of Maine). The Park Authority is not under the direct control of the governor or the legislature, though, and remains autonomous from other state agencies as well. A park superintendent, appointed by the Authority, is the chief administrator.

In Baxter's later years, he established a trust fund to provide capital for the Park's continuing operation. Baxter State Park receives no public monies for its operation, the one exception being the Perimeter Road, which is maintained with funds from the state highway department. Otherwise, the Park relies entirely on the trust fund and the entrance and camping fees. The governor's plans were well thought out and provided for all contingencies. His love for this land and recognition of its unique natural features led him down an unparalleled path culminating in the protection of a remarkable domain for all to see and enjoy.

The human history surrounding Baxter State Park is colorful, but its natural history is no less so—and it is considerably longer and more awe-inspiring.

The natural history of the area began approximately 500 million years ago, when the accumulation of sediments from shallow seas formed the sedimentary bedrock that today remains the Park's oldest rock. Following this, volcanic activity produced the mountains in the northern section of the Park. Millions of years later another period of volcanic activity created the bedrock in the southern half of the Park, including Katahdin. Then a long period of erosion began reshaping the land and forging the shapes of today's mountains. Not until the Ice Ages were the mountains' basic forms altered.

Glaciation put the finishing touches on the landscape. In some places, the land was scraped into a featureless terrain, but in other areas the glaciers carved into the bedrock an array of spectacular formations. The jagged peaks and sparkling ponds that endear the Park to so many visitors are the result of the advances and retreats of the ice sheets. The retreating glaciers also left in their wake a community of arctic plants and animals that today survives in Katahdin's alpine zone.

Weathering and erosion from wind and water are the principal players that today slowly alter the landscape, although occasionally a landslide will quickly transform a limited area. The other major player that today affects the Park is fire.

After the ice sheets retreated, the land here eventually developed a lush growth of forest supporting a variety of wildlife. But the Park's virgin boreal and northern hardwood forests vanished with the arrival of the lumberjacks. Since the drastic alterations made by the lumbering industry, however, the Park's forests have bounced back, testifying to the amazing resiliency of the Maine woodlands, but it will be a long time before these forests again resemble the original ancient stands.

Today, still in the process of recovering from the extensive lumbering, Baxter State Park stands as the preeminent example of wilderness in New England—and perhaps the entire eastern United States. Thanks to the insight and resourcefulness of one man, Katahdin will forever shine as a bright beacon in an ever-shrinking sea of wilderness. Percival P. Baxter put it this way: "Man is born to die. His works are short-lived. Buildings crumble, monuments decay, and wealth vanishes, but Katahdin in all its glory forever shall remain the mountain of the people of Maine."

High Peaks
and
Alpine Zones

Many different species of lichen grow on the barren, windswept North Traveler Trail. Lichens are nonflowering plants composed of fungi and algae coexisting in a symbiotic relationship. They are extremely hardy and consequently are quite common above treeline.

An exemplary wilderness area, Baxter State Park embodies a complex of ecosystems and natural features of stunning beauty and great significance. Out of this diverse mix of natural wonders, the mountains emerge decisively as the Park's dominant features. The lofty summits of Baxter State Park set this region apart from the surrounding landscape: Nowhere else in Maine is there such a massive collection of high alpine peaks. Not only do the mountains provide visitors with the very best of the Park's most-used form of outdoor recreation (hiking), but the mountain's alpine zones contain some of Maine's, and New England's, rarest plants and animals.

Baxter State Park's mountains can be divided into two groups: Katahdin and its surrounding peaks, in the Park's southern half; and The Travelers, with their associate mountains, in the Park's northern confines. There are distinct differences between the two mountain regions in age, origin, and composition.

More than 500 million years ago, during the early part of the Paleozoic era, most of eastern North America was covered by shallow seas, which remained for approximately 200 million years. Sediments of sand, mud, and the shells of marine invertebrates were slowly deposited on the ocean floor, where they accumulated and compacted to form sedimentary rock. The sedimentary bedrock covering the area north of Trout Brook is the Park's oldest rock.

About 400 million years ago, during the Lower Devonian period of the Paleozoic, in what is now the northern part of Baxter State Park, a series of volcanic islands formed in the shallow sea where the aforementioned sedimentary rock was developing. These islands resulted from the accumulation of lava flows and volcanic ash beds and formed the rock that we know now as Traveler rhyolite.

Rhyolite is an igneous rock formed by the cooling of the molten material known as magma. Traveler rhyolite is an excellent example of *extrusive* igneous rock (i.e., rock formed as lava solidifies at the earth's surface). It is a fine-grained dark grey or black rock, occasionally banded with light-colored veins of different minerals.

Successive lava flows left a mass of rhyolite over the existing sedimentary rock in the ancient sea bed. Approximately eighty cubic miles of rhyolite were formed, sometimes to depths of several thousand feet, making this one of the largest volcanic deposits of this type in the world. The rhyolite covered the width of the present-day Park and the area from Trout Brook south to the Wassataquoik Lake area. North of Trout Brook remain the sedimentary shales, slates, and sandstones of the early Paleozoic, and south of Wassataquoik Lake lies the much younger Katahdin granite.

After the volcanic activity ceased, the seas retreated, followed by a slow process of erosion that reduced the mighty lava-spewing volcanoes to mere stumps. The mountains in the northern part of the Park are the eroded remnants of those ancient rhyolite volcanoes. The Traveler is the largest, a grand mountain with several long, rocky ridges radiating out from its barren summit. To the west, across the waters of the South Branch Ponds, rises Black Cat Mountain. Northwest of The Traveler are a group of rhyolite peaks called the Deadwater Mountains—Bald, Billfish, Horse, and Trout Brook mountains—beautiful peaks accented by remote ponds that fill the depressions between them.

The sediments resulting from the erosion of the rhyolite volcanoes were deposited along Trout Brook and its tributaries, leaving a band of sandstones

Ring lichen (Parmelia centrifuga) *growing on a slate slab north of Trout Brook Farm. Ring lichens spread outward from a central rosette that dies with age while new growth continues on the margins, forming the unusual round patterns.*

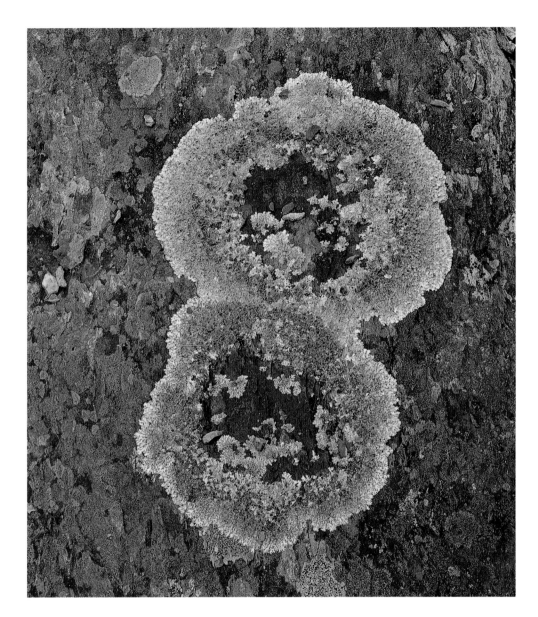

and conglomerates over that part of the Traveler rhyolite. At a later geological date, a tilting of the land to the north further hastened the erosion process and caused the folding of the sedimentary rock layers north of Trout Brook.

Columnar jointing, an interesting feature of the Traveler rhyolite, is observable in several of the area's rock outcrops. Columnar jointing results when specific conditions are present while lava is cooling, causing it to contract in a certain way. This contraction caused the Park's rhyolite to form five- or six-sided columns that are so distinct in some areas that they resemble the hand-carved stone pillars of ancient palaces.

After the formation of the Traveler rhyolite, rock-forming volcanic activity ceased for about 60 million years, until the Middle Devonian period of the Paleozoic era, when new volcanic activity created Katahdin and its surrounding mountains.

Katahdin is the magnificent zenith of Baxter State Park's superb mountainscape. It is Maine's highest mountain, attaining an elevation of 5,267 feet. This massive rock monolith towers over the flat, lake-dotted country to the south. Viewed from the west however, Katahdin is the culminating peak in a long chain of peaks that the Indians called *Katahdinauguoh*. From south to north, The Owl, Barren, O-J-I, Coe, South Brother, North Brother, and Fort mountains make up this range. To the west of the Katahdinauguoh is Doubletop Mountain, and to Katahdin's east are the Turner mountains. When viewed from the east, Katahdin appears as a series of peaks separated by huge, rounded valleys. From each direction, Katahdin has a different appearance, yet it always commands a dominating position in the landscape.

The rock that forms Katahdin is the Park's youngest. About 360 million years ago, during the Middle Devonian period, a huge dome of magma rose from the earth's depths and intruded into the sedimentary bedrock above, becoming the heart of an immense volcanic complex. When activity ceased, granite, an intrusive igneous rock, was formed by the cooling magma below the earth's surface. This granite is of a specific composition known as Katahdin granite.

Katahdin granite, which makes up the bedrock of Baxter State Park's southern half, has two distinct types: a grey form that predominates at the lower

Visible along the North Traveler Trail's open ledges are examples of columnar jointing in outcrops of Traveler rhyolite. Beyond lie Upper South Branch Pond and Black Cat Mountain.

The precipitous headwall of the South Basin, showing Pamola and Chimney peaks. The prominent ravine running from the headwall's base to a point between the two peaks is a couloir called The Chimney. This is a favorite route of rock climbers, who need rope and technical equipment to negotiate the several large chockstones that block this otherwise open couloir.

and middle elevations, and a pink form found only at higher elevations. The color variation is the result of different colored feldspars, a mineral that accounts for approximately 60 percent of the granite's composition. The grey granite contains mostly white feldspar while the pink type's feldspar is predominantly pinkish. The pink and grey granites cannot always be distinguished due to the effects of weathering and a lush growth of lichens that often mask the granite's true color.

Another interesting feature of Katahdin granite is the existence of numerous cracks, known as joints, wherever an outcrop occurs. The joints were formed in one of two ways: either by contraction as the magma cooled, or by the force exerted upon the joint by the rock in which the magma intruded.

Chimney Peak and the Knife Edge, viewed from Pamola Peak. Clearly evident is the jointing in the Katahdin granite that promotes the weathering responsible for many of Katahdin's spectacular geological formations.

The joints make the granite brittle and also promote weathering by allowing in moisture that causes fracturing as it freezes and thaws. Many of the outcrops are split by multiple joints running in different directions. When this rock breaks, it fractures along these joints to form angular blocks with smooth, flat surfaces. The fractured remains of these blocks litter the slopes of Katahdin, often in sizable boulder fields. The weathering of the jointed outcrops has produced some of the Park's fabulous scenic features, such as the large rock slabs on Katahdin's Cathedral Trail.

The creation of Katahdin granite marked the end of rock formation in the area that Baxter State Park occupies. Next began a 350-million-year period during which the region's soft, sedimentary rock was eroded by streams and rivers. As the fresh water carried the layers of sedimentary rock to the sea, the harder, more resistant igneous rocks of Katahdin granite and Traveler rhyolite were left exposed, forming the basic shape of today's mountains in Baxter State Park.

These mountains were further modified by the effects of glaciation, which

Along the Appalachian (Hunt) Trail on Katahdin's Tableland are many interesting formations, such as these large parallel slabs of Katahdin granite.

began about one million years ago during the Pleistocene epoch. At least four times during that period, enormous ice sheets covered a substantial part of the Northern Hemisphere, including Maine. About 25,000 years ago, glaciers of the late Wisconsin age were the last ice sheets to sculpt the bedrock of Baxter Park.

Glaciers—large masses of ice that move across the land—are formed when the yearly accumulation of snow exceeds the yearly rate of melting. Consequently snow builds up and is compressed by its own weight, creating glacial ice. Along the glacier's leading edge, where ice meets bedrock, its tremendous weight creates enough friction to melt the ice.

*The fracturing of granite along its weak joints has resulted in countless boulders that blanket Katahdin's upper slopes. The Katahdin granite's pink color is masked by a lush growth of map lichen (*Rhizocarpon geographicum*) which gives the rock a greenish cast.*

Glimpsed from the Northwest Basin Trail near the Saddle, Chimney Pond is dwarfed by Pamola Peak and the Knife Edge.

As water flows out and refreezes, the glacier then slides along.

The glaciers that engulfed the region that today is Baxter State Park were thousands of feet thick. They thoroughly blanketed the entire Katahdin massif—as shown by the occurrence of erratics on Katahdin's summit. Erratics are pieces of rock transported by a glacier from one area to another, sometimes over considerable distances. Some of the erratics on Katahdin's summit are fragments of bedrock from areas north of the St. Lawrence River.

Katahdin's alpine zones are Maine's only location for the rare bearberry willow (Salix uva ursi). The plants are either male or female, identified by their catkins. This specimen is a male.

The stunted, misshapen trees that grow near or above treeline are known as krummholz. Their small size is no indication of their age, which often is well over a century.

*Lapland rosebay (*Rhododendron lapponicum*) is a low-growing arctic plant graced with beautiful magenta blooms in early June. Katahdin has Maine's only habitat for this plant.*

*Mountain Sandwort (*Arenaria groenlandica*) is an abundant species that blooms in July. It often grows in disturbed areas close to footpaths.*

Late afternoon light spreads a glow over the sedges and rushes on Katahdin's Tableland. The Tableland encompasses Maine's largest alpine habitat and harbors more rare plant species than any other single location in the state. North Brother Mountain is in the distance.

High Peaks and Alpine Zones

Katahdin is Maine's only location for alpine bearberry (Arctostaphylos alpina)*, a low-growing member of the heath family. The new green berries turn black with age, while its leaves turn fiery red in autumn.*

Moss Plant (Cassiope hypnoides)*, one of Katahdin's rarest plants, is found in wet ravines or slopes above treeline. When not in bloom, it very much resembles the mosses among which it grows.*

Glaciers reshape the land by fracturing underlying bedrock through the melting and freezing of water, which seeps into crevices in the rock. Furthermore, as these fragments of rock are dragged by the moving ice, they scour the bedrock below. As glaciers advance, rocks, gravel, and other ice-embedded debris carve the bedrock into a variety of glacial features—from huge cirques in the mountainsides to small striations on the surfaces of rock outcrops.

The period of glaciation came to an end when the climate warmed, causing the glaciers to melt. As they shrank, they deposited great amounts of debris from their abrasion of the bedrock, forming numerous glacial features. This type of glacial deposit is known as drift. Unstratified drift is debris directly deposited by a glacier, with all particle sizes mixed together; stratified drift is material transported from glaciers by meltwater streams and then deposited, often in sedimentary layers sorted by particle size. Baxter State Park has a variety of glacial features created by the sculpting of the rock and the subsequent deposition of drift.

Among the principal Park features produced by continental glaciation are U-shaped valleys carved out of the bedrock by the advancing glaciers. These valleys, characterized by steep walls and a broad floor, have a distinct U shape when viewed from either end. They are obviously very different from the V-shaped stream-eroded valleys. Most of the large valleys in Baxter State Park are U-shaped. One of the finest, extending from Russell Pond to Roaring Brook Campground, has a broad, flat floor bordered by the steep sides of Katahdin and Russell Mountain to the west and the Turner Mountains on the east.

Another type of glacier-produced valley is a cirque. Cirques and their associated features are among the most spectacular geological formations in Baxter State Park. They are carved by valley glaciers occupying the sides of a mountain. In a process called frost-wedging, meltwater from a glacier makes its way into cracks in rocks and freezes, causing the rock to break off and be carried away by the glacier. This is the primary way that a glacier forms a cirque, which is characterized by a steep

Sunset bathes Katahdin while clouds form over the Knife Edge.

headwall and sides forming a broad, bowl-shaped valley. A cirque often looks like a giant horseshoe deeply carved into the side of a mountain. Baxter Park's Great Basin, South Basin, North Basin, and Northwest Basin are quintessential examples of cirques. On the floor of most cirques is a small body of water, known as a tarn, that fills the depression left by the weight of the glacier. The South Basin's exquisitely formed cirque cradles Chimney Pond, Baxter's best-known glacial tarn.

Glacial moraines are another natural phenomenon that occurs at the mouth of many cirques. Moraines are unstratified drift deposits of coarse material that accumulates at the end of a glacier. When a glacier's rate of melting at its terminus equals the rate of its forward movement, the glacier's end is stationary, but the ice within the glacier continues to advance and move material. The result is an accumulation of debris at the stalled end, creating a coarse pile of rubble—a moraine. The clear waters of the Basin Ponds fill depressions behind Baxter Park's largest glacial moraine. More than two miles long and over fifty feet high, it is a result of the glaciers that carved the

Great Basin. Glacial moraines are common throughout the Park, but they are not always evident. At the mouth of the North Basin, for example, is a small pile of boulders named Blueberry Knoll— this is probably the Park's best preserved and most easily discerned example of a glacial moraine.

A striking feature sometimes associated with valley glaciers and cirques is an arête, which occurs when the headwall or valley walls of a cirque erode to an extremely narrow ridge. Hamlin Ridge is an arête that formed between the valley glaciers that occupied the North Basin and the Great Basin. The Knife Edge, arguably Baxter Park's most notable and striking feature, is an extraordinary example of a glacial arête. Almost a mile long and only several feet wide in some places, with precipitous 1,500-foot drops on either side, it is without question the most breathtaking geological phenomenon in the eastern United States.

Valley glaciers persisted on the cooler upper slopes of Katahdin even after the the continental ice sheet retreated from the surrounding lowlands between 9,000 and 15,000 years ago. Consequently, the cirques and other

features formed by valley glaciers are the Park's most recent evidence of glaciation.

As the climate warmed and the glaciers retreated, so did the arctic plants and animals that inhabited the cold, inhospitable zone near the edge of the ice sheet. Their populations gradually shifted northward, to what is today's arctic zone. Some arctic species, however, still survive in isolated areas south of the arctic zone. At high elevations, arctic conditions persist even at temperate latitudes. Katahdin's high, barren, windswept slopes, with a mean annual temperature of only 30° F, provide the conditions required by these organisms.

Today, within the Park, communities of arctic plants and animals persist in the alpine zones of The Traveler, Fort Mountain, North Brother Mountain, and, of course, Katahdin. The bulk of the Park's alpine habitat is on Katahdin. The enormous ice sheets of the past sheared off Katahdin's top, leaving a broad, plateaulike expanse known as the Tableland. The Tableland lies above treeline at elevations between approximately 4,300 and 4,700 feet. Here, in Maine's largest expanse of alpine habitat, are alpine communities that harbor about thirty species of alpine plants. One of the rarest plant communities in the northeastern United States, it also contains the largest concentration of rare plants in Maine.

Treeline occurs on Katahdin at about 4,000 feet. At this point, trees of normal size give way to a treeless zone. Sometimes the demarcation is abrupt, but more often there is a transitional growth of dwarfed, stunted trees known as krummholz. On Katahdin, the krummholz consists primarily of balsam fir (*Abies balsamea*) and black spruce (*Picea mariana*). The poor, thin soils and short growing season at high elevations causes the trees to become dwarfed, and Katahdin's high winds further limit growth by shearing off branches and twigs. The krummholz often takes on bizarre shapes as it grows away from the prevailing winds, making it occasionally look like bonsai shrubbery adorning Katahdin's bleak slopes.

The krummholz trees are temperate-zone species that grow to normal height at lower elevations. They adapt to near-arctic conditions by growing close together in tight groups and taking on an almost horizontal shape to limit their exposure to the elements. True alpine tundra plants have evolved similar modifications that enable them to thrive in alpine zones.

Alpine plants are small and frequently grow in such sheltered areas as

*Diapensia (*Diapensia lapponica*), one of Katahdin's loveliest alpine flowers, often grows in large masses, covering slopes with its dainty white blooms each June.*

rock crevices. Some species form dense mats close to the ground, while others grow in very tight, self-protective clumps. They usually have tough stems and branches and very small, leathery leaves. The conditions tolerated by these plants are similar to the dry conditions of a desert. Although annual precipitation is high, the plants make little use of this water. Neither Katahdin's thin soils nor its boulder fields and rocky slopes hold moisture well. In addition, the relentless winds promote evaporation and rob plants of moisture. The alpine plants' leathery leaves and compact shapes prevent water loss.

As elevation increases, krummholz gives way to the dwarf shrub heath community—dwarf species that occasionally form great mats. Low sweet blueberry (*Vaccinium angustifolium*) and alpine bilberry (*Vaccinium uliginosum*) are two common heaths that produce delicious fruit in late summer. Lapland rosebay (*Rhododendron Lapponicum*) is a low, mat-forming, evergreen heath that in early summer produces stunning bright pink flowers similar to cultivated azaleas and rhododendrons. One of Katahdin's most beautiful flowering al-

pine species, it is found nowhere else in Maine. Not all of the plants in this community are true alpine species, however. Low sweet blueberry and such other plants as Labrador tea (*Ledum groenlandicum*) and pale laurel (*Kalima polifolia*) also grow at much lower elevations.

Sedges and rushes combine with the dwarf shrubs and heaths at Katahdin's higher elevations, creating another type of alpine community known as the sedge-rush/dwarf shrub heath community. The ground cover here is composed primarily of alpine reindeer lichen (*Cladonia alpestris*) and a number of haircap mosses (*Polytrichum* spp.). Emerging from the ground cover are Bigelow's sedge (*Carex bigelowii*) and highland rush (*Juncus trifidus*), with dwarf shrubs and heaths scattered about. The sedges and rushes superficially resemble grasses (although they are actually quite different), giving this community a more meadowlike appearance. The shrubs found here include two rare alpine willows, bearberry willow (*Salix uva-ursi*) and dwarf willow (*Salix herbacea*), the latter being the rarer of the two. Katahdin is the only known location of these

plants in Maine. Another rare shrub found here is the dwarf birch (*Betula glandulosa*), the smallest of the alpine birches, which grows in bushy clumps at several locations on the Tableland.

Above the sedge-rush/dwarf shrub heath community, near where the Tableland slopes up to Hamlin Peak, is a true meadow community. Highland rush is the dominant plant, covering the area in a glimmering sea of grass reminiscent of a western prairie.

In Katahdin's dry, rocky areas, alpine plants find refuge among the stones and boulders in what are known as fellfield communities. A variety of lichens, predominantly map lichen (*Rhizocarpon geographicum*), cover the rocks, while dwarf trees and shrubs and several types of moss are found between the rocks. Fellfield communities are also good areas in which to look for Lapland rosebay.

Snowbank communities are found on the leeward side of slopes and rocks as well as in depressions where winter's snowfall accumulates. The snow that builds up protects the plants from winter's severity. The late-melting snow, however, delays growth until late May or early June. Some of Katahdin's rarest alpine plants are found in snowbank communities. They are, for example, the state's only site where moss plant (*Cassiope hypnoides*) and mountain heath (*Phyllodoce caerulea*) grow. Moss plant is a delicate plant that superficially resembles moss but actually is a member of the heath family. If it were not for its small, white, bell-shaped flowers, the plant could easily be mistaken for a moss. Mountain heath also resembles moss but it sports lavender, urn-shaped flowers. Both burst into bloom early in the growing season, when the snow begins to melt.

On Katahdin are some inhospitable barren sections where vascular plants cover 50 percent or less of the ground. Diapensia (*Diapensia lapponica*), the predominant plant in these areas, is a small evergreen that grows in a dense clump resembling a pincushion. Diapensia is widespread on certain areas of the

*Alpine azalea (*Loiseleuria procumbens*) is a rare, petite alpine plant that grows close to the ground in small mats. Its tiny pink flowers bloom during early June. Katahdin is its only location in Maine.*

Tableland. Its small white flowers, which usually appear the second week of June, blanket the rocky terrain with a conspicuous, warming glow. Also found within these diapensia communities are alpine azalea (*Loiseleuria procumbens*) and alpine bearberry (*Arctostaphylos alpina*). Alpine azalea, a small member of the heath family, has tiny evergreen leaves and small, pinkish, bell-shaped flowers. Alpine bearberry is a low-growing plant that spreads in mats and produces green berries that turn black with age. In autumn, its deciduous leaves turn a brilliant red.

Mountain sandwort (*Arenaria groenlandica*) is another common alpine species. Like diapensia, it grows in small, dense tufts and is covered with white flowers in early July. Although it is found in a variety of alpine communities on Katahdin, it seems to favor disturbed areas such as those bordering many of the mountain's footpaths. The brilliant

The North Basin is Mount Katahdin's most perfectly formed cirque. Its impressive U shape is clearly evident from the top of its towering headwall.

white flowers fringe the paths like reflective lines along a highway.

In addition to the previously mentioned uncommon species, Katahdin is host to a number of other alpine plants that are even rarer. The star-like saxifrage (*Saxifraga stellaris*), one of the rarest plants in Baxter State Park, is found nowhere else in the eastern United States. The arctic-loving willow (*Salix arctophila*) is common in the arctic, but in the eastern United States it occurs only at one location on Katahdin.

Katahdin's alpine zone also is a refuge for a number of other arctic organisms, including several insects. The most celebrated of these is a small butterfly, the Katahdin arctic (*Oeneis polixenes katahdin*). It was separated from its parent species the Polixenes arctic of the far north, during the retreat of the region's last glaciers. It survived on Katahdin's summit and developed into a unique subspecies that is found nowhere else in the world. This rather nondescript creature has drab colors that camouflage it superbly within its alpine-meadow habitat. The Katahdin arctic butterfly's flight begins during July, but its cryptic coloration makes it somewhat difficult to spot.

The northern bog lemming (*Synaptomys borealis*) is a four-inch-long rodent with a short tail, tiny eyes, and inconspicuous ears. It is common in the arctic zones of northern North America, but in Maine it has been recorded only on Katahdin. This rare, elusive animal is not restricted to Katahdin's alpine zones; it also occurs in the mountain's spruce forests and bogs.

The water pipit (*Anthus spinoletta*) is a sparrow-size songbird common in the alpine zones of the far north. Its only known nesting site in the eastern United States is on Katahdin. Each year, usually on the Tableland, a small number of these birds raise their young. Although they are primarily insectivorous, they have been observed eating corn chips offered by hikers. Their drab brownish color is not particularly exciting, but what they lack in flashy colors they make up for with song. During the breeding season, male pipits exuberantly practice an aerial display in which they rise, almost vertically, 50 to 150 feet, sweetly uttering weak, paired notes—*che-wee, che-wee, che-wee, che-wee*.

Katahdin is an important refuge for rare alpine organisms but it also is home to all the more familiar residents of the northern forests and mountains, so it is an ideal spot for observing wildlife. Katahdin is the breeding ground for many species of common birds in addition to the rare water pipits. White-throated sparrows (*Zonotrichia albicollis*) and dark-eyed juncos (*Junco hyemalis*) nest amid the Tableland's krummholz and boulders and are almost constantly within sight or sound of summer hikers. Another of Katahdin's conspicuous avian denizens is the common raven (*Corvus*

corax), frequently seen soaring in the mountain's rising thermal air currents while uttering its guttural cries.

In winter, on the Tableland, tracks of the snowshoe hare (*Lepus americanus*) are abundant, giving evidence of a rodent other than the northern bog lemming. The hare tracks often form dizzying patterns, indicating a propensity for seemingly pointless travel. Summer hikers regularly encounter moose (*Alces alces*) in the high cirques. Occasionally, black bear

(*Ursus americanus*) are seen foraging on the abundant crop of blueberries produced in late summer on Katahdin and the Park's other mountains.

Those who explore Katahdin and the other mountains of Baxter State Park will encounter a world of unlimited beauty with a dazzling array of plants and wildlife. Successive visits, instead of being redundant, will continue to provide an ever-new display of natural wonders.

Ponds,
Streams,
and Bogs

Blue flag iris (Iris versicolor) is common along pond margins and in such wet areas as this fog-enshrouded marsh near Daicey Pond.

FOREVER WILD

Baxter State Park, home to Maine's greatest mountains, also has its share of beautiful ponds. From the summit of Katahdin, the Park's maze of mountains and dense forests is broken by the glimmering surfaces of the many ponds and streams, which create a striking mosaic of land and water. The Park's aquatic domains are of impressive beauty and include large, deep lakes; small, secluded ponds; surging mountain streams; and spongy bogs.

The glaciers that forged Baxter's most impressive mountain features were also responsible for the ponds that dot the landscape here. The crushing weight of the enormous continental ice sheets compressed the land below. When the glaciers retreated, the ground sprang back in an uneven fashion, resulting in myriad depressions. These depressions then filled with water, forming shallow ponds or bogs. As the glaciers began to melt, large blocks of ice sometimes broke loose and remained behind, while drift deposits

Dawn's glow illuminates North Turner Mountain and the tranquil waters of Russell Pond.

from the receding glaciers built up around them. When these ice blocks melted, their depressions formed ponds known as kettles or kettleholes. Many of the Park's small, circular ponds—such as Russell Pond, Rat Pond, and Round Pond—are kettles.

As discussed in the previous chapter, tarns also have glacial origins, having been associated with cirques. The sculptural effects of a valley glacier, drift deposits, and the depression caused by the glacier's tremendous weight all combine to form this type of pond on the floor of a cirque. Baxter State Park's glacial tarns include some of the loveliest ponds in this region. Their crystal-clear waters and remote locations, cradled within the glacier-carved rock, embody a pristine wilderness unique in the eastern United States. These tarns, although of inestimable scenic value to hikers, are much less significant for wildlife. The deep penetration of ice in winter renders the ponds incapable of supporting fish, and in summer they suffer from limited food supplies.

Chimney Pond, the Park's best-known tarn, lies in the South Basin. It is embraced by a precipitous headwall more than 1,500 feet high that features Pamola

Peak, South Peak, Baxter Peak, the Cathedral Arête, and the serrated top of the Knife Edge.

Lake Cowles and Davis Pond are tarns of provocative beauty on the floor of the remote Northwest Basin—unquestionably one of the Park's wildest areas.

Klondike Pond is a seldom-visited spot of similar beauty and spirit. Lying at an elevation of 3,435 feet, it is the Park's highest body of water.

The pond-forming glaciers have long gone, yet each year new ponds appear here courtesy of nature's preeminent engineer, the beaver (*Castor canadensis*). With the exception of man, no animal is better equipped than the beaver to alter its environment. Lured by a current of flowing water, beavers compulsively dam the flow to create a pond where they store food, construct living quarters, and raise their young. In addition, the beaver pond creates an entirely new habitat that attracts and supports a variety of mammals, birds, insects, and plants. Eventually, the beaver pond silts up and the beavers move on to a new waterway. Left behind in the silted pond is a developing meadow, which provides yet another habitat for animals and plants.

Beavers are common in the Park and play a key role in maintaining biological diversity within the woodlands.

The distinction between a lake and a pond is not always precise. Generally, a lake is a large standing body of water whose water temperature changes with depth, and a pond is a smaller, shallower body of water whose temperature remains relatively uniform. But many exceptions exist, usually the result of an unusual geological event—such as a landslide in a deep ravine that dams water into a small, deep pond. Lake Cowles, for example, has a relatively small surface area but a depth of fifty-two feet.

Three very large bodies of water in the Park fit the definition of a lake: Nesowadnehunk Lake, of which a small portion lies within the western border of the Park; and Webster Lake and Grand Lake Matagamon, both in the northern section of the Park. Grand Lake Matagamon, with a surface area of 4,165 acres, is by far the largest. (The majority of the Park's waters are small ponds with surface areas of less than a hundred acres.) The water levels in Matagamon Lake and Webster Lake are maintained artificially by dams. During the lumbering era,

Beaver (Castor canadensis) *are common aquatic mammals whose extraordinary dam-building abilities are responsible for the creation of many small ponds in the Park.*

many of the ponds and streams were dammed, but these dams are now gone, and most of the waters are now at natural levels.

The ponds of Baxter State Park are of exceptional scenic value. They are also an important habitat for a variety of plants and animals. For example, the Park's waters are home to a number of fish species. Brook trout (*Salvelinus fontinalis*), common throughout the Park, are the prize sought by most fishermen. Landlocked salmon maintain populations in Webster and Matagamon lakes. An introduced population of Sunapee char (*Salvelinus alpinus*) exists in the South Branch Ponds. This extremely rare fish was left landlocked in Maine's ponds during the last period of glaciation. Its relative, the Blueback char (*Salvelinus alpinus oquassa*), another rare species

Each of Baxter Park's ponds is an oasis of biological diversity amid the unbroken boreal forest. They attract and support a variety of plants and animals, adding to the diversity of species in the forest. The forest-dwelling moose (Alces alces) depend on the pond's aquatic vegetation as an important dietary supplement.

The setting sun's last golden rays shower Davis Pond and Harvey Ridge, in the Park's remote Northwest Basin.

stranded by the glaciers, can be found in Wassataquoik Lake.

A variety of water birds frequent the ponds. The plaintive, yodeling cry of the common loon (*Gavia immer*) is particularly familiar. A true wilderness inhabitant, the loon is happily at home in these remote waters. The gaudily colored drake wood duck (*Aix sponsa*) and its mate

breed alongside the quiet woodland pools. Great blue herons (*Ardea herodias*) and American bitterns (*Botaurus lentiginosus*), long-legged waders, frequent the shores of Park ponds in search of fish or frogs. Another common breeder is the spotted sandpiper (*Actitis macularia*), a tiny shorebird that is especially fond of the ponds and lakes with gravel beaches,

where, with tail constantly flittering, it patrols for tiny invertebrates.

There are few reptile species in Baxter Park waters. The largest, the snapping turtle (*Chelydra serpentina*), is a highly aquatic species that rarely leaves the water except to breed. It feeds on both plants and animals, including fish, frogs, and birds.

Reptiles may be scarce but amphibians are abundant. Just after the snow melts, the Park's shallow ponds swarm with legions of spring peepers (*Hyla crucifer*), tiny woodland tree frogs. Their high-pitched trills vociferously herald spring's arrival. The most common frog in Park waters is the green frog (*Rana clamitans*), found in company with its relative the mink frog (*Rana septentrionalis*). A north-woods species that is close to the southern limit of its range in Baxter Park, the mink frog is named for the minklike odor produced by its skin when handled roughly. Other Park frogs

Chimney Pond is an exquisite glacial tarn on the floor of the South Basin. On clear mornings, sunlight strikes the precipitous rock walls that form the South Basin cirque, giving the pond a spectacular backdrop.

White-tailed deer (Odocoileus vir-ginianus*), although not as common as their larger relative, the moose, are frequently spotted around the Park's ponds.*

include the northern leopard frog (*Rana pipiens*), the pickerel frog (*Rana palustris*), and the wood frog (*Rana sylvatica*). The American toad (*Bufo americanus*) is a common amphibian that wanders the forest floor, only returning to water in the summer to breed.

When the spring peepers enter the ponds, so too do the spotted salamanders (*Ambystoma maculatum*). Terrestrial throughout the year, they breed in the ponds early each spring. The closely related blue-spotted salamander (*Ambystoma laterale*) also dwells in the Park. While these salamanders favor quiet waters for breeding, the two-lined sala-mander (*Eurycea bislineata*) is at home year round in the cool, flowing waters of the Park's mountain streams. Additional species of salamanders are found throughout the Park; although seldom seen, they are very common.

The lakes and ponds also attract a variety of mammals. Some, such as the river otter (*Lutra canadensis*) and mink (*Mustela vison*), are permanent residents, while others, such as the white-tailed deer (*Odocoileus virginianus*), visit the ponds only to feed or drink.

Probably the Park's best-known pond visitor is the moose (*Alces alces*). During the summer, moose nearly submerge themselves in their attempts to flee the relentless attacks of black flies and mos-quitoes. Their primary reason for fre-quenting the ponds, however, is to feed on the lush aquatic vegetation. Like other herbivores, moose develop a sodium imbalance as a result of their steady diet of woody plants. The chemical makeup of certain aquatic plants helps correct this imbalance. The ungainly moose—a rather comical creature to watch as it goes about its business—is the animal that to most people typifies the Baxter State Park wilderness.

Besides creating ponds, the glaciers also redirected stream courses by eroding new channels in bedrock or by blocking them with drift deposits. It is believed that in preglacial times, Katahdin Stream (the headwaters of which flow from Witherle Ravine on Katahdin's north-west side) flowed into Nesowadnehunk Stream. In the vicinity of Katahdin Stream Campground, retreating glaciers blocked the course of the stream with an esker, a drift deposit that redirected Katahdin Stream into the West Branch of the Penobscot River.

Throughout Baxter are numerous eskers that have altered drainage systems since the most recent glacial period.

Moose (Alces alces) often perform comical feats in their search for food. Almost total submersion also provides relief from biting insects.

Katahdin, seen from Sandy Stream Pond, lights up in a blaze of snow-capped autumn color at sunrise.

Eskers are stratified drift deposits that accumulated in tunnels bored through the base of a glacier by meltwater. As the glacier melts, sand and gravel trapped in its ice are deposited in the tunnels, eventually resulting in a sand and gravel ridge that marks the former course of the meltwater stream. Eskers are characteristically long, narrow, winding ridges 10 to 150 feet high and sometimes more than 100 miles long. The most conspicuous esker here extends from the Togue Ponds to Abol Pond. The first three miles of the Park Perimeter Road are constructed along the top of that esker.

A small section of the East Branch of the Penobscot River runs through the northeastern corner of the Park. This river and one of its tributaries, Webster Stream, drain the Park's northern section and are Baxter's only large rivers.

Most of the waterways consist of rugged mountain streams and their numerous small tributaries. There are three major mountain stream systems. Nesowadnehunk Stream drains the

Sunrise over Grand Lake Matagamon, in the Park's northeastern section.

western side of the Park from Nesowad-nehunk Lake south into the West Branch of the Penobscot; Trout Brook drains the northern and central areas into the Penobscot's East Branch; and Wassata-quoik Stream is the primary watercourse draining the central and eastern Park areas—also into the East Branch. Sandy Stream is a smaller watercourse that drains most of the water from the Great Basin.

Many of the streambeds are noted for their huge boulders. Even at the streams' highest flood levels, these boulders are much too large to have been brought here by the flow of water in the present drainage system: They could only have been deposited by the glaciers and the torrents of glacial meltwater that were strong enough to transport such monsters. The finest example of this phenomenon is the South Branch Pond delta, which separates Upper South Branch Pond from Lower South Branch Pond. Before the delta was created, the ponds were a single body of water. The delta was formed by the accumulation of sediments at the mouth of Howe Brook, whose headwaters are high on Traveler Mountain.

Most of the major waterways are graced with beautiful waterfalls, cas-cades, and quiet pools. The waterfalls of Baxter Park are a varied mélange, ranging from delicate spills to gushing cascades. Katahdin Stream Falls, one of the most spectacular, is found along Katahdin Stream, where it tumbles through a deep ravine in an eighty-foot drop. Along the nearby Nesowadnehunk Stream are two major falls close together—Big and Little Niagara Falls—each with a volumi-nous spill of water emptying into a large, deep pool. In the central region, Wassa-

A cow moose (Alces alces) *and her calf feed in Sandy Stream Pond.*

taquoik Stream passes through a long ravine of fractured Katahdin granite in what is called Grand Falls. An exceptionally beautiful spot is Green Falls, where a small stream from the top of Wassataquoik Mountain plunges precipitously through a lush, mossy ravine into Wassataquoik Lake below.

The northern section of the Park also has its share of waterfalls. The Grand Pitch along Webster Stream is a spectacular fall and cascade spilling through a narrow slate canyon. Near Traveler Mountain, Howe Brook has two sets of beautiful falls but probably is best known for its exceptionally well-shaped potholes, which are formed by pebbles and stones caught in whirlpools. Over the years, their constant abrasion bores deep, round, smooth-sided holes in the bedrock. Potholes come in a variety of sizes and are found in almost all of the Park's streams.

South Branch Falls, along South Branch Pond Brook, is an interesting cascade that plunges through a channel of large slabs of Traveler rhyolite. There are also several well formed potholes in the stream's bedrock.

Besides its lovely falls, South Branch Pond Brook boasts a number of other interesting geological features. During the Lower Devonian Period, the area's rhyolite volcanoes began to erode. The first particles of rhyolite to break off were large, and they helped form the sedimentary rock—conglomerate—that was deposited on top of the bedrock of Traveler rhyolite. As the volcanoes eroded to rounded hills, only finer-grained sand and gravels were deposited. This was followed by a tilting of the land to the north. The newly accumulated sands slid northward and formed a layer

*Two young bull moose (*Alces alces*) battle during the autumn rut.*

of sandstone, on top of which developed a swampy plain where muddy sediments were deposited to form shales on top of the sandstone.

South Branch Pond Brook, from its origin at South Branch Pond to its confluence with Trout Brook, carves an interesting channel through these sloping sedimentary layers, providing a unique trip through time by exposing rocks varying in age from the oldest rhyolites at the stream's beginning to the youngest shales near Trout Brook. A short distance past the Traveler rhyolite at South Branch Falls, the stream exposes the conglomerate layers. Farther on, it cuts through the layers of sandstone and shales, revealing fossils of ancient shallow-water invertebrates. Fossils in this area are composed primarily of shell

Steep-sided mountain walls surround the cold, clear waters of Wassataquoik Lake, one of the Park's wildest and most stunningly beautiful bodies of water.

Grand Falls, on Wassataquoik Stream, is an impressive torrent of cascading water.

FOREVER WILD

fragments of Brachiopods—marine animals that, despite their superficial resemblance to clams, are in fact quite different. As many as ten species of Brachiopods have been identified here. Farther downstream, in the shales of the Trout Brook Valley, are fossils of vascular plants. Many species of these have been identified, with most dating to the Middle Devonian period more than 350 million years ago.

Bogs are among the most unusual of Baxter State Park's aquatic resources. Most of the bogs here are poorly drained areas of wet, spongy ground that fill glacial kettleholes, but others occur along the margins of certain ponds and streams where similar conditions exist. Whereas a mountain stream's swift current or a spring running into a pond brings nutrient-rich silts and replenishes the

South Branch Falls tumbles through several rock slabs of Traveler rhyolite.

In early spring, the distinctive ribbed green leaves of false hellebore (Veratrum viride) can be found growing along Trout Brook.

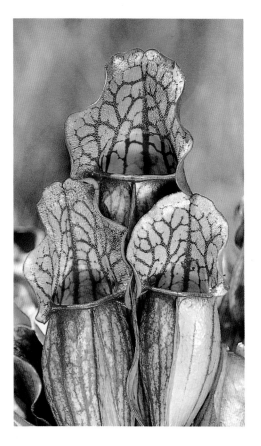

The leaves of the carnivorous Northern Pitcher Plant (Sarracenia purpurea) are water-filled traps that secrete a nectar to lure insects to their death.

Blooming sheep laurel (Kalmia angusti-folia) and bracken ferns (Ptiridium aquilinum) flourish along the outer margins of one of the Park's larger bogs.

Fossils of brachiopods, marine invertebrates over 400 million years old, are found in the exposed sedimentary rock along South Branch Ponds Brook.

Leatherleaf (Chamaedaphne clyculata) *is a bog shrub that in early summer produces dainty, bell-like flowers.*

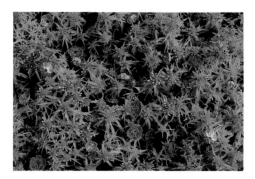

Sheep laurel (Kalmia angustifolia) *petals lying atop the bog's bed of sphagnum moss* (Sphagnum *spp.*).

water's supply of dissolved oxygen—both necessary for the growth of animals and plants—bogs are stagnant areas that lack the necessary flow of oxygen and food. In addition, their highly acidic water cannot support the growth of the bacteria responsible for decomposition, so bog vegetation does not decay but instead accumulates as peat. The sterility of a bog's peat layers is legendary. Timber from fallen trees has been removed from bogs in excellent condition after being submersed for hundreds of years. Bogs have also been known to preserve the remains of animals, centuries old.

The most characteristic features of the bogs are their spongy mats of sphagnum moss (*Sphagnum* spp.—the sphagnum genus contains a number of species that are rather difficult to distinguish). Special cells in the sphagnum's leaves are able to absorb up to sixteen times their own weight in water, making these plants well suited for existing on a water-logged surface.

Despite the generally inhospitable conditions in a bog, a variety of plants and animals have adapted to life there. Some of the more interesting plants grow on top of the floating sphagnum mats, and all of the plants have devel-

oped various strategies for survival. Some plants have even become carnivorous, extracting much-needed nitrogen from the proteins of their insect prey. In Baxter State Park, the Northern Pitcher Plant (*Sarracenia purpurea*) is the most conspicuous of these carnivorous plants. Its insect-catching ability lies within the specialized rosette of leaves at its base. The leaves—fleshy, tube-shaped structures with a thick ruffled lip—act as pitchers to collect rain water. Glands on the lip secrete a nectar that attracts insects, usually flies. An insect that enters the "pitcher" is trapped by short, bristly hairs that point downward and prevent its escape. The insect then drowns in the rain water, where nutrients released by its decomposition are absorbed by the plant. In midsummer, pitcher plants produce a single red flower on a leafless stalk. The plant's large flowers drop quickly, but the umbrellalike style sometimes lingers through winter, further increasing this unusual plant's oddity.

The carnivorous sundews are also common in the Park's bogs. The round-leaved sundew (*Drosera rotundifolia*) is the most abundant, but the similar spatulate-leaved sundew (*Drosera leucantha*) also occurs in some areas. Sundews are

Rhodora (Rhododendron canadense) is an unusual member of the heath family in that it is deciduous. In spring, before its leaves expand, it bursts into a blaze of blossoms that flush the bogs with their distinctive pink hue.

small, delicate plants that grow among the sphagnum and produce small, white flowers atop a leafless stalk in summer. The Sundew's leaves are covered with thick, glandular hairs beaded with a sticky liquid. Insects that become stuck in the hairs are gradually enfolded by the leaf and digested.

The horned bladderwort (*Utricularia cornuta*) is a carnivorous plant that grows in large groups at the edges of bogs and ponds. Its bright yellow summer flowers brighten the dull grasses and moss of its environs. These plants suck very small organisms into hollow sections on their underwater roots, where the organisms are then digested.

Orchids, too, have adapted to the harsh life of the bog. In order to obtain necessary nutrients, the orchids depend on a symbiotic relationship with fungi of the Mychorrizae family. The fungi live on the orchids' roots and act as substitutes for the bog's missing bacteria by

The rose pogonia (Pogonia ophio-glossoides), an uncommon orchid, is found in several of the Park's bogs.

The bog copper (Epidemia epixanthe) is a small butterfly restricted to the bog habitat, where its larvae feed on a plant known as the wren's egg cranberry (Vaccinium oxycoccos).

FOREVER WILD

decomposing organic material and supplying nutrients to the orchids. Orchids are among the bog's most beautiful plants and include a number of species.

Rose pogonia (*Pogonia ophioglossoides*) and grass pink (*Calopogon tuberosus*) are two charming pink orchids found in several bogs in the southernmost parts of the Park. The white-fringed orchis (*Habenaria blephariglottis*) also occurs in some of these bogs. There are several other species of orchids in the Park's bogs, but they are less showy than the three mentioned above.

The perimeters of many bogs support a lush growth of heath shrubs. They manage to thrive in these inhospitable conditions thanks to several adaptations. For example, their leathery or waxy leaves prevent moisture loss, and therefore they need to absorb very

*The yellow flowers of horned bladderwort (*Utricularia cornuta), *a carnivorous plant, border the boggy margin of Tracy Pond.*

On the Appalachian Trail's ascent of Katahdin, the footpath passes spectacular Katahdin Stream Falls.

little of the harmful acidic water that surrounds them.

Leatherleaf (*Chamaedaphne calyculata*) a common heath with small, white, bell-shaped flowers, colonizes the sphagnum mats, often forming a dense growth. Labrador tea (*Ledum groenlandicum*) is also a dense, low-growing shrubby plant with terminal clusters of white flowers that appear in May and June. Sheep laurel (*Kalmia angustifolia*) and its smaller relative the pale laurel (*Kalmia polifolia*) brighten the bog with their showy pink flowers around the same time that the Labrador tea blossoms. The heaths' most spectacular floral display occurs during the first week of June, when the rhodora (*Rhododendron canadense*) burst into bloom, blanketing the bog or pond margins with a glorious vibrant pink hue.

The two species of trees that are most readily at home in Baxter's bogs are the tamarack (*Larix laricina*) and the black spruce (*Picea mariana*). Tamaracks are especially attractive in mid-October, when the deciduous needles of this conifer species turn a brilliant yellow.

Besides the hordes of biting flies and mosquitoes that frequent the bogs, a number of more aesthetically appealing insects make their home in this habitat. Several butterflies are good examples. The bog copper (*Epidemia epixanthe*) is a tiny creature whose larvae feed on the wren's egg cranberry (*Vaccinium oxycoccos*), which grows among the heaths. This butterfly occurs in small numbers and never leaves the confines of the bog. The bog fritillary (*Proclossiana eunomia*) is far rarer in the Park and not often seen. One of its host plants is the Alpine Bistort (*Polygonum viviparum*), one of Katahdin's rarest arctic species.

Too often regarded as unattractive wastelands, bogs in fact are among the most specialized and intriguing communities of the northern forest. With few exceptions, the bogs of Baxter State Park are successional communities that will succumb eventually to the encroachment of the surrounding woodlands. As the heaths and conifers take anchor in the sphagnum, the bog will be replaced by a coniferous forest. In a northern climate, however, this process can take hundreds, even thousands, of years.

The Forests

*A red maple (*Acer rubrum*) and bracken ferns (*Ptiridium aquilinum*) in their distinctive fall wardrobe.*

From the air, the mountains of Baxter State Park appear to rise through a blanket of green that enwraps even the highest peaks almost to their summits. This green sea reaches as far as the eye can see. These boreal forests, dark and untamed, are populated by spruce and fir, whose dense evergreen canopies make the woodland floor a damp, light-starved world.

The Park's forests are composed primarily of conifers: red spruce (*Picea rubens*), black spruce (*Picea mariana*), and balsam fir (*Abies balsamea*). Other conifers that occur in suitable habitats but to a much lesser degree include white pine (*Pinus strobus*), red pine (*Pinus resinosa*), eastern red cedar (*Thuja occidentalis*), and tamarack (*Larix laricina*).

The spruce-fir forest is dominant in Baxter Park because those trees are specifically adapted for life in these climatic conditions. The conifers, with their evergreen needles, are able to perform photosynthesis over a longer period than deciduous trees, which drop their

*The dense, dark, and mossy boreal forests of Baxter State Park are dominated by red spruce (*Picea rubens*) and balsam fir (*Abies balsamea*).*

leaves each autumn. Some conifers even continue photosynthesis in temperatures that hover around the freezing point. The conifers' cells are able to reduce their water content and increase their concentration of sugars to form a resinous fluid that acts as an antifreeze in the frigid air. Their needles are thick and fleshy to retain moisture that otherwise would be robbed by the forest's unremitting winds. Conifers have flexible branches that resist breakage under the weight of snow or when winds turn severe.

The single greatest factor of change in the forests since the last glacial period was the lumbering that began in the mid-nineteenth century. Only a few virgin stands of wood presently survive, among them the sizable stand on The Traveler near the headwaters of Howe Brook. A more accessible stand, located between the North Basin and the Basin Ponds, is one of Maine's finest examples of old-growth red spruce. Many of the trees in this area are well over three hundred years old. In the summer of 1990, another area of old-growth red spruce was discovered on North Turner Mountain. Core samples indicate that the trees are quite ancient, with one specimen estimated at 423 years.

The Park's largest stand of virgin wood lies in the large glacial bowl of The Klondike, between Katahdin and the mountains of the Katahdinauguoh group. Lumberjacks avoided this wet, boggy depression, where the dominant species is the bog-loving black spruce.

An interesting phenomenon of the spruce-fir forests occurs on the mountain slopes ringing the Klondike: long, narrow bands of dead wood form a curious striped pattern among the living trees. These striking patterns, known as fir waves, have been the subject of much debate. They seem to occur in parallel bands at different elevations—almost a living topographic map of the mountain's contours. Balsam fir, the prevalent tree in this area, appears to reach a certain age or height and then die. The trees are knocked over by wind or snow, and new growth takes their place. When the new trees reach a certain height, the process of change begins again, and the band of dead wood shifts up the mountainside. Although the cause of this is not fully understood, it may be related to underlying deposits of coarse, rocky material that seem to parallel the mountain's contours. One theory suggests that a fir wave might start along these bands, where mature trees, finding it difficult to absorb moisture and stay rooted, eventually die. Baxter State Park is the only Maine location of fir waves, but they have also been observed in other areas, including small examples in New York's Adirondack Mountains and the White Mountains of New Hampshire. Fir waves are also known in Newfoundland and northern Japan.

Even though the dense evergreen growth blocks most of the sun's rays from the forest floor, the conifer understory supports an amazingly lush carpet of mosses and lichens. Rocks and decaying logs are sometimes densely covered, looking rather like plush green pillows on the forest floor. Several species of clubmosses, resembling tiny trees, form their own miniature forest. Sides of cliffs and

boulders support growths of polypody ferns (*Polypodium vulgare*), which mantle the rocks with their evergreen fronds. Above, bearded lichen (*Usnea cavernosa*) droops from the limbs of spruce and fir like living tinsel on a Christmas tree.

This moist green carpet is home to a number of flowering plants. In June, the flowers of bunchberry (*Cornus canadensis*) appear. This is a low-growing, abundant

*Raindrops cover a spiderweb draped over a red spruce (*Picea rubens*) bough.*

*Fir waves are curious growth patterns of balsam fir (*Abies balsamea*) found on the mountain slopes surrounding The Klondike, here viewed from The Owl.*

plant that in some areas blankets the forest in a white sheet of blooms. By late summer, it produces a cluster of red berries, further adding to its charm. Goldthread (*Coptis groenlandica*), only three to six inches high, has a solitary white flower that appears very early in spring. Its name comes from the bright golden color of its threadlike roots. Another common plant in this habitat is the starflower (*Trientalis borealis*). Like the previously mentioned species, it is small, only four to eight inches in height. It is a charmer, however, possessing delicate white flowers arising from a whorl of glossy leaves. Bluebead lily (*Clintonia borealis*) is noted for its beautiful but poisonous blue berries, which are far more conspicuous than its unusual green flowers.

One of the loveliest plants in this forest is the pink lady's slipper (*Cypripedium acaule*), a large woodland orchid. Its single flower rising from a leafless stalk

*Balsam fir (*Abies balsamea*) seedlings grow among a carpet of twinflower (*Linnaea borealis*) on the forest floor. A member of the honeysuckle family, twinflower has a sweet scent that fills the summer air.*

looks very much like an inflated pink slipper. Baxter State Park has an abundance of a rare white variant of this species; the pink form, which is more common in other areas, is scarce here.

Each year, the boreal forests play host to a fabulous array of breeding songbirds. The fiery red throat patch of the male Blackburnian warbler (*Dendroica fusca*) can sometimes be glimpsed as this bird works the treetops for insects. The Cape May warbler (*Dendroica tigrina*) is a common songbird that favors the spruce forests. Also abundant are the yellow-rumped warbler (*Dendroica coronata*) and the magnolia warbler (*Dendroica magnolia*). The woods come alive each spring with the song of approximately twenty-three breeding warbler species. Warblers that breed in the conifers avoid direct competition for food by engaging in a kind of resource partitioning—each species feeds in a certain part of the tree. For instance, Blackburnians feed at upper

*Bunchberry (*Cornus canadensis*) is a common wildflower in Baxter State Park. What appear to be white petals are actually bracts that surround the plant's minute true flowers. Its early blossoms produce red berries by late summer.*

levels, while the yellow-rumps make use of the lower limbs.

The gray-cheeked thrush (*Catharus minimus*) inhabits the spruce and fir at higher elevations. This shy bird of the north woods is related to the American robin (*Turdus migratorius*), but it lacks that bird's bright-colored breast. In early morning and again at dusk, the gray-cheeked fills the woods with a stirring, ethereal song.

Occupying the spruce near the mountain summits is the tiny boreal chickadee (*Parus hudsonicus*), a year-round Park resident that braves all but the most severe winters. The chickadees show little fear of humans, and their curiosity sometimes leads them to approach quite closely. Another Park resident that makes itself right at home with humans is the gray jay (*Perisoreus canadensis*). It is common throughout the Park but especially visible in the area around Daicey Pond. These bold birds will steal food from an unsuspecting hiker or camper in the blink of an eye, and very often can be persuaded to eat right out of a hand.

The remote boreal forests are home to the spruce grouse (*Dendragapus canadensis*), a large, chickenlike bird. Also called "fool's hen," it is uncommonly tame, allowing close approach by humans. As a result, it was once hunted relentlessly for its meat. This, combined with habitat loss, has made the bird quite rare, but it still persists within the Park in small numbers.

And then there are the birds of prey. The most common is the broad-winged hawk (*Buteo nitidus*). Often seen along the Park Perimeter Road, it perches in a tree to await the appearance of an un-

*A red squirrel (*Tamiasciurus hudsonicus*) peers from its nest hole in the trunk of a tree.*

*The American toad (*Bufo americanus*) is a common woodland amphibian that patrols the forest floor in search of insects and small invertebrates.*

*The pine marten (*Martes americana*), a member of the weasel family, resides in the Park's deep forests. They are voracious hunters of small mammals and birds—red squirrels being their primary prey—but they also forage for carrion, berries, and seeds. The Park supports a healthy population of martens, but their elusive nature makes them difficult to observe.*

*The Canada mayflower (*Maianthemum canadense*), despite its name, blooms during June throughout Baxter Park, where its dainty blossoms carpet the forest floor.*

*The gray jay (*Perisoreus canadensis*) is a familiar bird around Park campgrounds, where it boldly steals food from unwary campers.*

suspecting chipmunk or snake. The sharp-shinned hawk (*Accipiter striatus*), Cooper's hawk (*Accipiter cooperii*), and northern goshawk (*Accipiter gentilis*) are swift, agile flyers that patrol the forests, preying on the songbirds and some small mammals. The peregrine falcon (*Falco peregrinus*), once native to this part of Maine, had not lived here for the better part of this century, but thanks to a persistent reintroduction program, a pair did successfully nest in the Park in 1989. When darkness falls, the barred owl (*Strix varia*) is the chief avian predator.

A striking autumn mosaic of hardwoods and conifers dominates the slopes of South Turner Mountain.

The Park has fine stands of northern hardwoods that blaze with color in autumn.

In Baxter State Park, the rare white form of the pink lady's slipper (Cypripedium acaule) far outnumbers its normally more common pink relative.

Vivid leaves of hardwoods litter the forest floor in a carpet of riotous color.

The Forests

Although it is rarely seen, its distinctive resonant whoo is one of the Park's most familiar nocturnal sounds.

Scampering about the forest floor and through the trees are the small mammals that make the north woods their home. The chattering cries of the red squirrel (*Tamiasciurus hudsonicus*) are everywhere in the spruce and fir forest. This squirrel is quite dependent on the annual crop of spruce cones as its major food source. It gathers the cones, carries them to a favorite spot, and shucks them for their seeds. The cone scales are left in a pile and the seeds are eaten or stored. It is hard to walk a trail in the Park without finding at least one of these telltale piles of shucked cones.

A healthy red squirrel population ensures the presence of one of its primary predators, the pine marten (*Martes americana*). This small, weasel-like mammal is dark brown, with a buff or orange throat patch, and somewhat resembles

*A single wild sarsaparilla (*Aralia nudicaulis) *emerges among a lush growth of long beech ferns (*Thelypteris phegopteris)*. Both species are abundant in the Park's woods.*

*Painted trillium (*Trillium undulatum*) is one of the Park's most attractive wildflowers. At lower elevations it blossoms in early May, but on higher mountain slopes it can be found blooming in late June.*

*This luna moth (*Actias luna*) was found seeking shelter from a storm in the krummholz bordering the treeline on Hamlin Ridge. It is one of several species of large, showy moths that inhabit the Park's forests.*

the mink (*Mustela vison*). It is opportunistic, snatching just about any type of prey available, and also eats berries, seeds, and carrion. The pine marten is quite inquisitive and often can be approached easily.

The pine marten's larger relative, the fisher (*Martes pennanti*), is a rather uncommon member of the weasel family that inhabits the Park. It is one of the few predators of the porcupines (*Erethizon dorsatum*). The fisher requires a large home range of undisturbed land, so Baxter is a perfect refuge for this true wilderness species. Other small animals common throughout the Park are the raccoon (*Procyon lotor*), red fox (*Vulpes vulpes*), and bobcat (*Felis rufus*).

Two blossoms of the wild strawberry (Fragaria virginiana) *peek out from a clump of northern blue violets* (Viola septentrionalis). *These common flowers appear in sunny openings in mid-May as the trees bud. The strawberry produces tasty fruit by midsummer.*

The moose (*Alces alces*) is the giant of the north woods. A full-grown bull can be as high as seven and a half feet at the shoulder and can weigh as much as 1,400 pounds. Its massive antlers regularly span four to five feet. In addition to its size, the moose is known for its somewhat comical features, which include long skinny legs and a peculiar muzzle that gives it a rather dopey look.

Although the moose frequents the Park's ponds to dine on aquatic vegetation, it is unquestionably a creature of the forest, where it finds shelter and protection. The tawny calves are born in late May or early June and remain with the mother until she drives them off before giving birth again the following spring.

A lush growth of polypody ferns (Polypodium vulgare) *carpets a boulder like hair on a head.*

Fewer than half of the cows give birth to twins; single-calf births are the norm. Autumn signals the breeding, or rutting, season, when bull moose become increasingly aggressive and occasionally battle each other for dominance of a cow. A bull will remain with a cow for a week or so before moving on to another female.

After watching the amusing adventures of a moose munching on plants or escaping bugs in a pond, or witnessing the tension of the rut when the big bulls battle for mates, it becomes evident why moose are such intriguing creatures.

The spruce and fir forests are interrupted by pockets of deciduous trees in places where conditions favor hardwoods —usually dry, warmer habitats. The sun-loving hardwoods also quickly colonize disturbed areas resulting from fire or disease outbreaks. They occupy these sites until conditions again favor the return of the climax forest of spruce and fir. (Climax forests are those in which species remain relatively unchanged over long periods of time.)

A bull moose (Alces alces) *finds a source of nutritious food among the hardwood saplings of a recovering burned-over area.*

Where the Park's spruce-fir forests were reduced by lumbering and lumbering-related fires, they have been replaced by a second growth of hardwoods. Baxter's most common hardwoods include American beech (*Fagus grandifolia*), yellow birch (*Betula alleghaniensis*), paper birch (*Betula Papyrifera*), sugar maple (*Acer saccharum*), red maple (*Acer rubrum*), green striped maple (*Acer pensylvanicum*), mountain maple (*Acer spicatum*), quaking aspen (*Populus tremuloides*), big-toothed aspen (*Populus grandidentata*), and speckled alder (*Alnus rugosa*).

Northern hardwoods allow more light to reach the ground than do their coniferous cousins, so there is a diverse understory of ferns and flowers. Several common shrubs inhabit this realm, including hobblebush (*Viburnum alnifolium*), a straggly plant that blankets the forest floor in some places. Its branches bend to the ground, where they take root and occasionally trip, or hobble, passersby. In early spring, it has clusters of white flowers that produce a reddish-black fruit relished by wildlife. Highbush cranberry (*Viburnum trilobum*) is a closely related species that grows among the hardwoods bordering the waterways, especially Nesowadnehunk Stream. It has early white flower clusters followed by edible red berries.

Each autumn, the hardwoods put on a spectacular display of color. As temperatures cool, trees prepare for winter by shutting down their flow of sap. At the base of each leaf's stem grows a layer of cells called an abscission layer, which cuts off the flow. The chlorophyll, used by the leaf for photosynthesis, quickly breaks down and dissipates. Other chemicals in the leaves—which are present all year but are usually masked by the green of the chlorophyll—are no longer hidden, and their flashy colors are revealed. Different species have different chemical makeups, resulting in the varying shades of yellow, orange, red, bronze, and purple that brighten the autumn landscape.

In early spring, ferns are almost the first greenery to poke through the ground's protective shield. Under some hardwoods, they are so abundant that they shroud the ground in green. The interrupted fern (*Osmunda claytoniana*), one such fern, appears early in spring and often occurs in masses. This large species bears its small, beadlike fertile fronds in the middle of its leafstalks, "interrupting" the parallel ranks of leafy fronds and producing a distinctive profile that inspired the plant's common name. The long beech fern (*Thelypteris phegopteris*) is a common delicate light-green plant that favors wet forest areas. Much less common, but also fond of wet, shaded woods, is the maidenhair fern (*Adiantum pedatum*), among the most beautiful and delicate of the Park's ferns. A good place to look for it is in the woods bordering Matagamon Lake. The spinulose wood fern (*Dryopteris spinulosa*) and the Christmas fern (*Polystichum acrostichoides*) are two evergreen ferns of the hardwood forests; the former grows in great abundance.

Under the hardwood canopy are numerous species of wildflowers. Two lovely denizens of the early spring woods are the painted trillium (*Trillium undulatum*) and purple trillium (*Trillium erectum*). The former, strikingly attractive, is far more abundant in the Park. The purple trillium, also known as stinking Benjamin, emits a foul smell that mimics carrion and attracts flies, which serve as pollinators. Wild sarsaparilla (*Aralia nudicaulis*) is widespread, often growing in extensive colonies. It has one leaf stalk and one flower stalk with several clusters of tiny green flowers. In autumn, its umbrellalike leaf flushes the woods with

a warm golden hue. Wild oats (*Uvularia sessilifolia*), a small plant with one or two drooping yellow flowers that bloom in early spring, is quite common through the Nesowadnehunk River valley on the Park's western side. Wild strawberry (*Fragaria virginiana*) is found throughout the Park, especially along the Park Perimeter Road. Its white flowers of spring develop a tasty fruit in midsummer that is relished by black bears (*Ursus americanus*) and humans alike.

Although black bear are common in any of the Park's varied habitats, they favor the hardwoods at certain times of the year. Autumn is one such time, when they prepare for winter by putting on as much fat as possible, feasting on the nuts of the American beech.

The hardwoods that replaced the conifers lost to the ax also created habi-

*The golden autumn leaves of striped maple (*Acer pensylvanicum*) and the brilliant white trunk of a paper birch (*Betula papyrifera*) stand out against a background of conifers. The seeds, buds, twigs, and bark of these northern hardwoods are important food sources for many of the Park's creatures.*

tat for white-tailed deer (*Odocoileus virginianus*). But white-tailed deer, unfortunately, carry a parasite that afflicts moose—a roundworm known as the meningeal worm. It damages the brain and nervous system of the moose, eventually paralyzing and killing it.

A fairly recent inhabitant of the Park's woods is the eastern coyote (*Canis latrans thamnus*). Coyote populations have been well established in Maine since the late 1960s, when coyotes, expanding their range in the west, arrived via Canada. This attractive animal, which weighs thirty to thirty-five pounds, is a year-round Park resident. Its thick, plush winter coat makes it appear so large that it often is mistaken for a wolf, which is not found in Maine. It eats just about anything, plant or animal, large or small —a major reason for its success. Although quite common, it is rarely seen and only occasionally emits the eerie vocalizations for which its western counterpart is famous. The keen-eyed hiker, however, will notice its scat and tracks almost everywhere.

Baxter State Park's forests are filled with other treasures too numerous to name. The woodlands are always alluring —a place to explore, a place to be immersed in a wilderness abounding in wonders of sight, sound, and scent.

The Park on Foot

The unusual triangular-shaped slide on the west face of Mount Coe is clearly visible from Old Jay Eye Rock on O-J-I Mountain. Mount Coe is accessible by a short but steep trail from the O-J-I summit.

Baxter State Park offers its visitors magnificent scenery, but because of its primitive wilderness, much of the Park can be observed only through the network of footpaths. The necessary hiking often requires strenuous physical exertion. Thus, preservation of the Park as a wilderness area—the very reason most people are drawn to it—also accounts for a certain amount of inconvenience for visitors.

The Park is open for general use (including overnight) from May 15 through October 15 and for day use from October 15 through December 1. It is open for day and overnight winter use from December 1 through April 1 (special rules apply) and for day use from April 1 to May 15. The outlying campsites of Chimney Pond and Russell Pond begin operations June 1 and end October 15. There are nine campgrounds with overnighting provisions (by reservation) that include tent sites, lean-tos, bunkhouses, and (at Daicey and Kidney ponds) cabins.

The best-preserved cirque in the Park is the North Basin. On its floor are two small ponds that are accessible by a short bushwhack from Blueberry Knoll.

All of the campsites and cabins are primitive. Water is available only from streams and ponds, there are pit toilets, and there is no electricity.

Day use for Maine residents is free. Out-of-state visitors are charged an automobile entrance fee. Overnight visits require reservations, which can be made in person at Baxter State Park Headquarters or by mail (not by telephone) no earlier than January 1. Reservations for overnight winter visits (minimum of four persons per party) are accepted beginning November 1. Reservation requests by mail should be made to:

Baxter State Park
Reservations Clerk
64 Balsam Drive
Millinocket, ME 04462

For more information, the Park number is 207/723-5140.

All of the campgrounds are accessible via the Park Perimeter Road, except for Russell Pond and Chimney Pond campgrounds, which are accessible only on foot. A number of remote campsites—tent sites and lean-tos—are available for overnight stays by backpackers.

Keeping Baxter Park in a natural state has meant forgoing the amenities provided in other parks and recreation areas. There are no hot-dog stands, souvenir booths, playgrounds, flush toilets, or telephones. Automobiles are restricted to the primitive Park Perimeter Road. The summit of Katahdin has no avenue of convenience like New Hampshire's road up Mount Washington. In order to stand astride Katahdin's lofty summit it is necessary to hike, climb, and scramble up its trails. Visitors are required to carry in their own food and carry out their trash (as of 1990, Baxter Park no longer supplies trash cans).

Although automobile access is limited, the Park has a fabulous network of well-maintained footpaths clearly marked by two-by-six-inch blue-painted blazes on trees and rocks. The Appalachian Trail is the one exception: It has white-painted blazes of the same configuration. On sections of trail above treeline, paint blazes are replaced by rock cairns, which offer greater visibility on the often fog-enshrouded summits.

Approximately 170 miles of trails extend into most regions of the Park and lead to a number of majestic peaks, shimmering lakes, and enchanting forests. Here hikers can appreciate the many subtle nuances of a flourishing natural community. Whether it be the plaintive

On Katahdin's exposed alpine summit, hikers are at the mercy of the weather, and there is no easy escape if conditions turn severe.

To keep hikers informed of conditions, the Park staff posts weather reports each morning at its gates and at campground ranger stations. The prevailing conditions are evaluated and authorities issue a class rating for each day. A Class I day means excellent conditions and good visibility, with all trails open to Katahdin's summit. On a Class II day, trails are open but not recommended for hiking because of potential weather deterioration. Class III means that the mountain is open but not recommended and one or more trails are closed because of weather conditions. On a Class IV day, all routes to the summit are closed. It is important to remember that even a pleasant Class I day can turn sour on a mountain like Katahdin, which is massive enough to produce its own microclimatic conditions independent of the area's prevailing weather.

All of the Park's trails merit exploration, and no trail should be avoided because it is not mentioned here. The trail descriptions that follow are intended only to spark interest and inspire enjoyment of the Park's footpaths. More detailed information on the trails appears in *Katahdin: A Guide to Baxter State Park and Katahdin,* by Stephen Clark. It is available at Park ranger stations, Park Headquarters, and bookstores.

There are trails of various lengths, difficulty, and character in Baxter State Park, including several outstanding one-day wilderness excursions. When considering high mountain trails, certainly the routes up Katahdin come to mind first. All of Katahdin's trails are exceptional, but certain ones stand out. The shortest routes start at Chimney Pond, which day hikers can reach from the Roaring Brook Campground. Alternatively, and possibly more rewarding, backpackers can spend several nights at 2,914-foot-high Chimney Pond Campground, using this as a starting point and eliminating the initial 1,500- to 1,800-foot ascent from the Perimeter Road to Chimney Pond before actually climbing the mountain.

One of the most popular circuit hikes from Chimney Pond is the 4.1-mile loop up the Cathedral Trail, on to Baxter Peak, across the Knife Edge to Pamola, then down the Dudley Trail, returning to Chimney Pond. This is undoubtedly the finest high-mountain hike east of the Mississippi, but the route is so boulder-strewn and steep that it would challenge the surefootedness of a mountain goat. The route is exposed for almost its entire distance, offering unsurpassed breathtaking views.

From Chimney Pond, this hike starts up the Cathedral Trail, which features three large rock outcroppings reminiscent of a fantastic Gothic cathedral. After this thrilling and strenuous climb, the trail joins the Saddle Trail, which follows a more moderate 1.7-mile route to Baxter Peak, the summit of Katahdin. Besides being the highest point in Maine, Baxter Peak is also the northern terminus of the Appalachian Trail. A large wooden sign marks the spot and indicates that the trail's southern terminus is in Georgia, a mere 2,135 miles away.

The next leg of the journey follows the Knife Edge Trail to Pamola Peak. This mile-long jaunt across a well-formed, narrow glacial arête is perhaps the Park's most legendary trail. The incredible Knife Edge is guaranteed to raise the awareness—and the blood pressure—of all those who traverse it. At certain points, the path is only a few feet wide, with precipitous 1,500-foot drops on either side.

Common goldeneyes (Bucephala clangula) breed in cavities of trees bordering many of the Park's ponds. This female is swimming across Sandy Stream Pond.

The Owl's snow-covered summit contrasts boldly with the colorful foliage on the slopes below. The Owl's summit offers hikers some of the Park's most impressive mountain scenery.

In three or four years, this five-month-old moose calf (Alces alces) may be as large as the full-grown bull beside him. These two were spotted in Sandy Stream Pond near Roaring Brook Campground, a reliable location for spotting moose.

The Park on Foot

Barrell Ridge, one of the rhyolite peaks to the northeast of The Traveler, can be reached from either South Branch Pond Campground or the Fowler Ponds Trail. It offers marvelous views, and delicious blueberries in mid-August. In the distance are Trout Brook and Billfish Mountain.

The views are spectacular, especially into the South Basin, where Chimney Pond is merely a shimmering speck on the land below. Due to the exposed nature of the Knife Edge, hikers must remain on the designated route at all times. It is foolhardy to attempt it in inclement weather, or even iffy weather. This is a slow-going route without shelter where a hiker is at the mercy of high winds, rain, sleet, snow, and lightning.

The Knife Edge leads to Pamola, Katahdin's easternmost peak, from which the descent along the Dudley Trail is steep and rocky. Although the footing can be tricky, the views are splendid. The Dudley Trail leads back to Chimney Pond, completing the circuit.

Another recommended hike from Chimney Pond is the 4.3-mile loop up Hamlin Ridge, a long, open arête that separates Great Basin from the North Basin. The route heads north from Chim-ney Pond on the North Basin Trail. A left turn at .7 mile begins the ascent along the Hamlin Ridge Trail. (A shorter climb involves continuing along the North Basin Trail, reaching the Blueberry Knoll moraine at 1.2 miles. There are excellent views here toward the Turners and the Great Basin, as well as the headwalls of the North Basin. It's also possible to bushwhack .2 mile through the scrub to the small ponds on the floor of the exquisite North Basin. This is a beautiful spot well worth the effort to reach.)

Hikers continuing up Hamlin Ridge quickly break out of the scrub and onto a long, exposed ridge that offers breathtaking views into the North Basin below. To the south, the Katahdin massif dominates, cradling the South Basin and Chimney Pond below. This is a magnificent perspective of Katahdin quite different from other viewpoints in the Park. At two miles, the trail reaches Hamlin Peak (4,751 feet), an extensive open area of alpine terrain with panoramic views.

From the summit, the trail descends slightly to Caribou Spring, named for the woodland caribou (*Rangifer tarandus*) that roamed Katahdin until their elimi-nation by hunting and habitat destruc-tion at the turn of the twentieth century. From the spring, the Northwest Basin Trail heads southward to join the Saddle Trail, a route that follows Katahdin's famed Tableland. Here, in early summer, the delicate flowers of alpine plants add a flush of color to the otherwise bleak landscape. Next, the route descends to Chimney Pond in 1.2 miles. The Saddle Trail, which has the most moderate grade of any of the trails accessible from Chimney Pond, is generally considered the easiest way up and down the mountain.

On the western side of Katahdin are two popular routes to the summit that start along the Perimeter Road. The Abol Trail, which begins at the Abol Campground, is the shortest route from the Perimeter Road to Baxter Peak, but what the trail lacks in length it makes up for in steepness. The trail very sharply ascends the Abol Slide, a long, open gash of loose stone and gravel, culminating on the Tableland at Thoreau Spring. From the spring, the trail follows the Appalachian Trail to Baxter Peak, arriving at the summit in 3.8 miles from the road—with an elevation gain of 3,982 feet.

From Katahdin Stream Campground, on the Perimeter Road, the Appalachian

(Hunt) Trail climbs 5.2 miles to the summit of Katahdin—a popular route with a series of outstanding scenic features. Katahdin Stream Falls, the first prominent feature along the path, is 1.1 miles from the campground. The 80-foot-high falls cascade through a picturesque, moss-covered ravine. At 2.8 miles, the trail abruptly leaves the woodlands and begins a difficult climb over and under boulders and rock slabs.

Next comes the ascent of the Hunt Spur, a long, open ridge of boulders resembling a towering pyramid of rocks.

From the spur, there are fabulous views in all directions. The climb up the spur leads to the Gateway, two large slabs of rock on either side of the path approaching the Tableland. The next feature is Thoreau Spring, named for the famed author, who visited this spot in 1846. From the spring (usually a reliable water source), it is one mile along the open expanse of Katahdin to Baxter Peak.

Katahdin's grandeur often overshadows other noteworthy peaks in the Park. In Katahdin's immediate vicinity are seven peaks that offer exhilarating hiking and interesting perspectives of their dominant neighbor: the Owl, O-J-I Mountain, Mount Coe, North Brother, South Brother, and Doubletop (all to the northwest of Katahdin), and South Turner (to the east). All of these peaks are exceptional and offer highly recommended hikes. Although these mountains are not as high as Katahdin, they should never be underestimated: All require steep climbs, and most of their summits are above treeline.

The Howe Brook Trail near the South Branch Ponds follows Howe Brook through a secluded wooded ravine with two sets of lovely falls.

The Owl, the conspicuous crest immediately to the northwest of Katahdin, is a splendid mountain sporting a marvelous southern face of precipitous rock. A 3.3-mile hike beginning at Katahdin Stream Campground leads to the summit (3,716 feet), from which there are exceptional views in all directions. Of special note is the vast bowl of The Klondike to the northeast. The Owl summit probably provides the best view of the Park's fir waves, the curious tree-growth patterns on the slopes surrounding The Klondike. Also from the summit of The Owl are views of some of Katahdin's most rugged terrain. Immediately to the south rises the imposing Hunt Spur; the untamed Witherle Ravine is ruggedly etched into the rock that slopes off Katahdin's Tableland.

O-J-I, another in the chain of peaks that encircles The Klondike, no longer deserves its name; a number of small

North of Trout Brook Farm, along the Freezeout Trail, are a series of flat slate ridges that are the oldest bedrock in the Park. Careful observation will reveal glacial striations—scratches on rock caused by the abrasion of moving glaciers.

The Wassataquoik Trail, which extends from Russell Pond west to the Park Perimeter Road, winds its way along the stunningly beautiful shores of Wassataquoik Lake. Passing gravel beaches, decaying snags, and rock slabs, the shoreline traverse is a wild, exciting, and beautiful route along an exquisite wilderness pond.

of loose rock, making the footing precarious. On the summit (3,410 feet), two knobs each provide fine views, but there is an even better view at Old Jay Eye Rock, reached along a side trail about five hundred feet north of the O-J-I summit. No one who climbs O-J-I should miss this short detour. To the north lies the densely wooded Nesowadnehunk Valley; to the northeast is Doubletop, commanding a regal position. There is also a fabulous view of Mount Coe and its western slide, which resembles a large cone of earth with a great gash branding its side.

For the energetic hiker, a mile-long trail starts just south of the O-J-I summit and leads to the 3,764-foot summit of Mount Coe, where there is a commanding view of The Klondike and its surrounding peaks. Farther north along the Mount Coe Trail is the junction with the Marston Trail, which begins on the Per-

slides have now made the original letter-shaped gashes difficult to distinguish. Two trails that ascend the slopes of O-J-I both begin along the Park Perimeter Road at Foster Field. Each follows a steep, rugged slide leading to the summit. A loop of 5.2 miles goes up the north slide to the summit and descends the south slide. On the north slide is an extensive area of steeply sloping rock polished by water coursing across its surface. The formation is spectacular, but it can be difficult to traverse in inclement weather. Both slides have an abundance imeter Road at the Slide Dam Picnic Area. The Marston Trail offers access to The Brothers, another pair of fine peaks. Both have open summits with unrestricted vistas. North of North Brother, continuing along the ridge of peaks surrounding The Klondike Bowl, is Fort Mountain (3,861 feet), which has an extensive alpine summit with remarkable views into Katahdin's remote Northwest Basin. Unfortunately, the ascent up Fort requires a difficult bushwhack from North Brother, as no trail is maintained to its summit.

Without a doubt, the dominant mountain in the western side of the Park is Doubletop, which is visible from numerous locations and appears as a massive pyramidal mound from most perspectives. Its neighboring peak, Squaw's Bosom, rests closely to the east, balancing Doubletop's striking silhouette. There are two routes up Doubletop, one starting from Nesowadnehunk Campground and the other from the Kidney

A short trail from the south shore of Wassataquoik Lake leads to Green Falls. The lower of the falls' two main drops spills its way through an enchantingly green mossy ravine.

Pond Camps Road. Each of the trails is a long, steep climb culminating in the double-peaked summit (3,488 feet at highest elevation) with excellent views in all directions. This is a highly recommended hike.

To the east of Katahdin lies a large mass of Katahdin granite crowned by three peaks: North, East, and South Turner mountains. A moderate two-mile climb beginning at the Roaring Brook Campground leads to the top of South Turner (3,122 feet), where a rocky knob provides a ringside seat for viewing the great cirques that are cut so deeply into Katahdin's eastern walls.

This mountainous southern half of Baxter Park also offers some wonderful low-level hikes through splendid woodlands. Besides being less strenuous, the Park's low-lying trails often afford the best opportunities for observing wildlife and wildflowers.

One of the most beautiful and untamed regions of the Park serviced by a trail is the Northwest Basin. Davis Pond, a shallow tarn on the floor of this cirque, nestles below its towering headwall. A nearby lean-to facilitates an overnight visit to this remote section of the Park.

From the Roaring Brook Campground, it is an easy .3-mile to the strikingly beautiful Sandy Stream Pond—one of the Park's most treasured features. South Turner Mountain rises dramatically above its northeastern shore, while Katahdin's sculpted granite form fills the horizon to the west. From this perspective on a clear morning, the sun's first rays bathe Katahdin in an ethereal glow that is reflected perfectly in the pond's calm waters. The fabulous vista from Sandy Stream Pond is quintessential New England wilderness.

As if that were not enough, Sandy Stream Pond's beauty is enhanced by a seemingly never-ending parade of moose (*Alces alces*) that come to feed on the pond's abundant supply of aquatic vegetation. This is one of New England's finest locations for observing moose carrying out their daily activities. Moose can be seen nursing their young, dodging the summer's biting insects, competing for mates, and conducting a variety of other fascinating behaviors. All this can be viewed comfortably from any one of the pond's numerous outlooks.

In addition, patient observers may spot white-tailed deer (*Odocoileus virginianus*), beaver (*Castor canadensis*), river otter (*Lutra canadensis*), red fox (*Vulpes vulpes*), and an array of other local inhabitants that make occasional appearances. The avian population is also varied and fascinating, with many species of songbirds frequenting the shores of the pond. Of special note are the white-winged crossbills (*Loxia leucoptera*). On summer mornings, the chattering song of winter wrens (*Troglodytes troglodytes*) echoes across the placid waters, and one never has to wait long for the rasping call of the belted kingfisher (*Ceryle alcyon*). Common goldeneyes (*Bucephala clangula*) can be seen rafting the waters as well as Red Breasted Mergansers (*Mergus serrator*) who have a special fondness for the abundant trout. For those with limited time in the Park, Sandy Stream Pond is a must.

Another easy path starting from Roaring Brook Campground is the Roaring Brook Nature Trail, which makes a .75-mile loop. It begins and ends near the footbridge over Roaring Brook, winding its way through a hardwood forest, a conifer forest, and a northern bog community. The bog, with views of Katahdin and South Turner Mountain offers all the flora and fauna one would expect to find in this type of habitat.

Klondike Pond is a wild, picturesque tarn in a deep ravine south of the Northwest Plateau. At an elevation of 3,435 feet, it is the highest pond in the Park. Unfortunately, there is no trail to the pond, so visitors must make a strenuous descent along a steep slide and bushwhack through scrub and around beaver ponds.

During the summer months, early risers at Russell Pond Campground will frequently encounter an eerily mist-covered pond.

This is an excellent place to observe the carnivorous round-leaved sundews (*Drosera rotundifolia*) and pitcher plants (*Sarracenia purpurea*), both abundant. In midsummer there is a wide variety of orchids in bloom. The pink rose pogonia (*Pogonia ophioglossoides*) is common here. The white-fringed orchid (*Habenaria blephariglottis*) is also rather prevalent. Birders should note that this is a reliable spot for the black-backed woodpecker (*Picoides arcticus*), which breeds here most years.

There are a number of similarly easy trails on the western side of Katahdin suitable for a half-day or full-day trek. One pleasant hike is the .8-mile trail to Little Abol Falls from Abol Campground. The small but charming waterfall, nestled in a picturesque ravine, spills gracefully down a fifteen-foot drop into a pool below.

Radiating from the Daicey Pond/ Kidney Pond region are several trails leading to other ponds and one that climbs a small mountain to the southwest of these ponds. The trail up Sentinel Mountain, an easy climb by Baxter Park standards, can be reached from Kidney or Daicey Pond. It is 3.3 miles from Daicey Pond, slightly less from Kidney Pond. The main summit of Sentinel is circled by a loop trail that offers vistas in all directions—including a view of Katahdin to the east and an inspiring view of Doubletop to the north. This hike is highly recommended for those desiring splendid mountain views with a minimum of effort. Among the other scenic ponds in this area is Rocky Pond, northwest of Kidney Pond, which is reached via an easy .6-mile trail. As its name suggests, boulders of various sizes are scattered about its shallow waters as if they had showered down from the summit of Doubletop, prominently situated across the water. This is one of the area's loveliest ponds and should not be missed.

The Lily Pad Pond Trail leads through a bog to a canoe landing on a small stream. A canoe must be paddled (park rentals are available through the Daicey Pond or Kidney Pond campground rangers) .25 mile along the stream to its convergence with Lily Pad Pond, a quiet body of water with a bog-lined perimeter. The views of Katahdin and the Park's other western peaks are outstanding.

From Daicey Pond, a loop hike of approximately five miles takes in the Appalachian Trail and Grassy Pond Trail and passes along the shores of Daicey, Elbow, Tracy, and Grassy ponds. These beautiful ponds offer exquisite views and are frequented regularly by Moose.

South Branch Pond Campground, in the Park's northern section, is the starting point for several wonderful trails. The North Traveler Trail and Center Ridge Trail ascend two different arms of The Traveler. They both require a good deal of climbing but reward hikers with tremendous views along their rocky, open ridges. In a deep notch between these two ridge trails lies the Howe Brook Trail, a pleasant hike along a mountain stream with two sets of beautiful falls.

The nearby Trout Brook Farm Campground is the starting point for the highly recommended 1.3-mile hike up Trout Brook Mountain. Despite a modest elevation of 1,767 feet, the views from the summit are outstanding.

The Park has a number of remote outlying sites for those desiring an overnight wilderness backpack. Russell Pond Campground, too, is accessible to

The last rays from the setting sun bathe Katahdin in a subtle glow above the stark frozen expanse of Kidney Pond. The few winter visitors who brave the deep snows and bone-chilling temperatures are often rewarded with unsurpassed wilderness vistas.

backpackers. One of the finest backpack trips in the eastern United States takes six days and makes use of the Russell Pond Campground.

The backpack begins at the Roaring Brook Campground and follows the Russell Pond Trail 7.1 miles northward to Russell Pond—a pleasant walk along the flat floor of a U-shaped valley. Right before Russell Pond, it's necessary to ford Wassataquoik Stream, which, during high water periods, can be a treacherous obstacle of gushing water and slippery rocks. Russell Pond, a beautiful spot with good fishing and plenty of moose, has tent sites, lean-tos, and a bunkhouse. An early arrival here affords time for an afternoon hike along the Lookout Trail. This 2.6-mile round trip climbs a low hill that has open ledges offering wonderful views of Katahdin off to the south.

The second day, the hiker follows the Wassataquoik Trail northwestward

to Wassataquoik Lake, 2.4 miles from Russell Pond. Gravel beaches and crystal-clear water flanked by steep-walled mountains make this one of Maine's most beautiful lakes. Adding further to the lake's appeal, the backpacker may spend the night in a small cabin on an island at the lake's eastern end. (Baxter Park keeps a canoe here for access.) Along the lake's southern shore is Green Falls,

considered by many to be the Park's loveliest falls.

On day three, the backpacker returns to Russell Pond and hikes the 5.8-mile loop to Ledge Falls and Grand Falls on Wassataquoik Stream. Grand Falls, especially impressive, consists of a cascade of water tumbling through a canyon of Katahdin granite. This trail passes through the sites of former lumber camps where old tools still may be found scattered about. Russell Pond is the camping place for this night as well.

Day four is a 5.3-mile climb southward along the Northwest Basin Trail to Davis Pond, in Katahdin's Northwest Basin. Along the way it's necessary to ford several streams, including Wassataquoik Stream. The Northwest Basin, the wildest and most remote section of the Park accessible by trail, is a magnificent glacial cirque with several tarns. Lake Cowles is the largest tarn, Davis Pond the second largest. The backpacker stays at the Davis Pond lean-to. (The outhouse at this lean-to has an open front with a striking view of the cirque's precipitous headwall.) It's possible to scramble up the talus slope above Davis Pond to a waterfall that empties into the pond—a wonderful spot to observe the cirque wall bathed in the setting sun's last rays.

On day five, the backpacker leaves Davis Pond and continues southward along the Northwest Basin Trail. The trail climbs out of the cirque almost vertically through a spruce forest until reaching treeline on Katahdin's Northwest Plateau. The plateau is an open, windswept extension of the alpine Tableland, with views in all directions. Caribou Spring is 2.3 miles away, after which it is an easy .2-mile hike to the summit of Hamlin Ridge, offering outstanding views of Katahdin. The trail continues along the Tableland and joins the Saddle Trail. From here, it is 1.2 miles farther to the night's destination, Chimney Pond. If time and weather permit, it is a 2-mile round trip from here to Katahdin's summit.

On day six the backpacker can explore Chimney Pond before hiking the 3.3 miles back along the Chimney Pond Trail to the starting point, Roaring Brook Campground.

Despite the deceptively short mileage, this trip is a physically demanding backpack, but unquestionably worth the effort. The trek is unique in that it traverses all of the varied habitats of the northeastern mountains.

Baxter State Park is utilized for other forms of recreation in addition to hiking and backpacking. Canoeing, for example, is popular, and rentals are available at several Park campgrounds. Fishing is excellent, and most of the Park's ponds and streams offer any angler a challenge. Challenges abound, too, for rock climbers. Mount Katahdin offers the Park's greatest rock-climbing challenge, with several routes beginning in the South Basin near Chimney Pond. Many climbers shy away from the brittle, loose rock encountered on summer climbs on Katahdin, preferring a winter ascent on the profusion of ice formed each year on the wall of the South Basin.

Winter use of the Park is strictly regulated. The Park Perimeter Road is not plowed, nor are the Park approach roads. Access is only by snowmobile or skis. Overnight winter stays are permitted, but participants must adhere to a stringent set of rules.

Winter's cloak presents the visitor with a far different Park from the one encountered during the summer months. Typically the snow cover reaches depths of four or more feet, and temperatures are often well below 0°F for extended periods. An overnight winter visit is demanding, but it nevertheless is an exhilarating activity offering great rewards.

Baxter State Park's network of footpaths traverses a variety of marvelous destinations and habitats, offering the hiker a rare opportunity to experience firsthand a portion of a dramatic but diminishing northeastern wilderness.

About the Photographs

The images in this book were made using a variety of photographic equipment and film. The majority of the landscape shots and some of the close-up subjects were photographed using a Zone IV 4x5 view camera equipped with 210mm and 90mm Schneider lenses. Kodak Ektachrome 100 Plus and Polaroid Prochrome 100 were the two types of sheet film used. Exposures were calculated using a Gossen Multi Pro hand-held meter.

I used a 35mm camera to capture the remaining subjects, including the animals, plants, and several landscapes. Two Canon F1 bodies fitted with a variety of Canon lenses, including the 500mm F4.5L, 200mm F4 macro, 50mm F3.5 macro, 20–35mm F3.5L, and the 80–200 F4L. A Vivitar 285HV flash came in handy on several occasions. Kodachrome 64 was the exclusive film for all 35mm subjects, and exposures were calculated with the F1's internal light meter and the Gossen Multi Pro meter.

A polarizing filter, an 81A warming filter, and a graduated neutral density filter were used occasionally. For all photographs, I used a Gitzo 210 tripod and an Arca Swiss monoball tripod head.

Acknowledgments

I would like to thank my editor, Karin Womer, and Down East Books for giving me the opportunity to realize this project. Thanks are also due to my sister, Judith Zygelman, for all her help, and to Don Riepe, of the American Littoral Society, for his assistance.

The Baxter State Park staff were most helpful whenever I visited the Park. I would especially like to thank Park Superintendent Irvin "Buzz" Caverly for answering many difficult questions; Chief Ranger Chris Drew for helping out with my first winter visit; and rangers Ester and Chris (at Chimney Pond) and Greg (at Roaring Brook) for directing me to many exciting locations. And I extend a very special thanks to Park Naturalist Jean Hoekwater for sharing her valuable time and assistance.

A tremendous thank-you goes to my hiking partners: Jeff Ritter, who daringly posed for numerous portraits along the Knife Edge while enduring the infamous black-fly assaults of early summer; Steve Vincent, for being crazy enough to accompany me up Baxter Peak, with full packs, for a sunset that never materialized; Walter Mugdan, who skied in with twelve pounds of frozen chili—the only edible dinner of the winter 1991 overnight trip—and then cheerfully cleaned the dishes; and Jonathan Frishtick, skier *par excellence,* who, along with Steve and Jeff, mirthfully survived subzero temperatures during our winter 1990 overnight.

I would also like to thank Mike McGrath, Tom and Susan Bushey, Andy Provost, Erik "Dunkan Jim" Rogers, and Bernard "Camp King" Zygelman for the hours of "intelligent conversation" while waiting for The Big One at Sandy Stream Pond.

Bibliography

AMC Field Guide to Mountain Flowers of New England. Boston: Appalachian Mountain Club, 1977.

Antevs, Ernst. *Alpine Zone of Mt. Washington Range.* Auburn, Maine, 1932.

Bennett, Dean. *Maine's Natural Heritage.* Camden, Maine: Down East Books, 1988.

Birds of North America. Washington, D.C.: National Geographic Society, 1983.

Blake. *The Animal Ecology of the Upper Slopes of Mount Katahdin.* Biological Monographs, vol. 10 no. 4, pps. 10–39. Urbana: University of Illinois, 1925–27.

Blake, Irving H. *Biotic Succession on Mount Katahdin. Appalachia,* vol. 18 (1931), pps. 409–24.

Caldwell, Dabney W. *The Geology of Baxter State Park and Mount Katahdin.* Department of Forestry Bulletin no. 12. Augusta, Maine, 1972.

Clark, Stephen. *Katahdin: A Guide to Baxter State Park and Katahdin.* Unity, Maine: North Country Press, 1985.

Eckstorm, Fannie H. *The Katahdin Legends. Appalachia,* vol. 16 no. 1 (1923).

Johnson, Charles W. *Bogs of the Northeast.* Hanover, New Hampshire: University Press of New England, 1985.

Klots, Alexander B. *Field Guide to the Butterflies of Eastern North America.* Boston: Houghton Mifflin, 1979.

Leavitt, Walter H. *Katahdin Skylines.* Orono: University of Maine at Orono Press, 1981.

Preliminary Vascular Flora of Baxter State Park. State Planning Office Miscellaneous Publication no. 37. Augusta, Maine, 1988.